MOTORWAY DRIVING

Expert advice and information
of Advanced

D1581723

KOGAN PAGE

INSTITUTE OF ADVANCED MOTORISTS MANUAL

The Editors gratefully acknowledge the assistance in compiling this book of many members of the examining and headquarters staff of the Institute, and of the IAM Council, including: Ted Clements, Courtenay Edwards, Terry Friday, Robert Peters, Michael Pickering, Michael Robotham, Brian Royle and Colin Thaxter. Thanks are due also to David Williams.

First edition published in 1988 by
Advanced Mile-Posts Publications Ltd
for the Institute of Advanced Motorists.

Revised edition published in 1989 by
Kogan Page Ltd,
120 Pentonville Rd, London N1 9JN
in association with the Institute of Advanced Motorists, IAM House, 359–365 Chiswick High Road, London W4 4HS.

The information given in this book is intended for general guidance only and to summarise the major provisions of the law. It is not intended as a definition of the law. Readers requiring legal advice or guidance are advised to consult a solicitor.

Printed and bound in Great Britain by Richard Clay Ltd, Bungay, Suffolk

British Library Cataloguing in Publication Data
Motorway driving. – Rev ed.
  1. Great Britain. Motor vehicles. Driving
  I. Institute of Advanced Motorists
  629.28'3'0941

ISBN 1 85091 915 1

CONTENTS

FOREWORD

The need for this book was first discussed at the Institute of Advanced Motorists, I understand, shortly after the Institute's former Chairman Michael Pickering had expressed the opinion in the Press that:

'Too many drivers do not understand motorways. Newly qualified drivers are scared of them, and experienced drivers often abuse them.'

He was correct then and, I am sorry to say, his views seem to be even more soundly based now, in the light of the many accidents, which are widely publicised, and which take place on what are supposedly the safest roads in Britain.

One school of thought is that swingeing punishment for offenders will improve the situation. I doubt it. The prospect of a heavy fine, loss of licence or even imprisonment is unlikely to be in the mind of a driver who makes a single mistake, or who commits an act of aggression, at 70 mph or more on the motorway – no matter how much the awful consequences of his act of folly may seem to justify harsh punishment.

If deterrent penalties are not the answer then what is? I agree with the Institute's view that the only hope lies in self-education: learning to be a better – and therefore safer – driver.

I know that this manual combines the knowledge and expertise of some of Britain's most experienced drivers, it is the first book specifically about motorway driving and as such should fill an empty space on any responsible motorist's bookshelf.

*By HRH The Duke of
Gloucester, GCVO
President of the Institute
of Advanced Motorists*

PART ONE

MOTORWAY DRIVING

1

WHY THIS BOOK?

The need for a book on motorway driving may not be immediately apparent. After all, it is generally accepted – by the Department of Transport, the police and the motoring organisations – that motorways are the safest of roads, so what is there for the IAM to worry about in its primary concern of road safety?

Motorways *are* our safest roads, but this is in spite of, not because of, the driving behaviour of many of their users. They are inherently safe on account of their dual carriageways, width and relative straightness, freedom from blind brows, the good surfaces, clear markings and hard shoulders. The value of the 70 mph speed limit in safety terms is a matter of opinion. The Institute has long felt that 80 mph would be a more natural limit, but the law must be respected – and, perhaps, should be enforced more vigorously.

The head-start of motorways over other roads is no reason for the conscientious driver to sit back complacently, switching the mind into neutral when driving on them. Motorways would be a lot safer still if everyone on them recognised their hazards, limitations and particular requirements, and drove accordingly.

Pie in the sky maybe, but trying to bring it down to earth is surely a worthy objective. The IAM has more than 85,000 members, all of whom believe that better driving means safer roads and that this can be achieved by sensible education. Apart from our membership, there are many other motorists who share our ideals of safety and good road behaviour and so are eager to improve their driving. *That* is why we decided to produce this book.

Britain's motorway network is now largely complete, embracing 1,853 miles of road (July 1988). More and more people are driving on it, so the time is right for a bit of intensive education on its use.

At the risk of seeming contradictory, let us say right away that there is more to motorway driving than just driving! To derive the maximum benefit from that network and keep out of trouble while not imposing it on others, you need more than just the basic ability to drive well.

Motorways are *special* roads. They have their own laws and lore, their own customs and codes of practice, their own conditions, all of which you should be familiar with and attuned to. One of those conditions is the relatively high speed of most of the traffic most of the time, which means that when an accident does occur it can be serious and involve a number of vehicles. Also some of those customs and practices do not make for the greatest safety. The IAM is well fitted to draw attention to some of the more dubious ones.

Through the years the Institute has evolved a philosophy of driving – a flexible philosophy based on the soundest possible principles and approved by the police and the insurance companies, among others. What we aim to do in these pages is to relate the problems of motorway driving to the IAM *ethos*, to explain why certain methods should be adopted.

Most drivers find their first few journeys on motorways quite frightening and a large number have never come to feel at ease on them, not least owing to the substantial number of fast-moving heavy goods vehicles. A bit of healthy respect is a great incentive to caution and sensible behaviour, but on the other hand would anyone really want a motorway driver to be like Hilaire Belloc's chamois who 'lives in perpetual fear'? Such timidity is exhausting and the exhausted driver must have an impaired performance, so one of our aims with this book is to banish the unnecessary fears while underlining the need for relaxed but constant vigilance.

We start with a look at the UK motorway system which may well contain several stretches that you did not know existed. The accompanying map is as up to date as we could make it.

Reference has already been made to the special laws that apply to motorway usage, and they are explained in detail in Chapter 3. The following chapter is a broad analysis of how the established IAM techniques are applicable to motorway driving, after which we go from the general to the particular in focusing on various important aspects of such driving.

Chapter 5 concentrates on joining and leaving the motorway, and Chapter 6 on what happens in between. You may think it slightly illogical to discuss leaving techniques before those actually needed on the motorway. We are assuming, though, that you will not be reading this book as you drive! Hence it is reasonable to integrate the 'on' and 'off' sections since they have a common factor – the slip road – which introduces the same sort of hazards into both operations.

Some of the emergencies that can occur on motorways are common to other roads as well, while others are what might be called indigenous. While the latter types are the main theme of Chapter 7 they are not its exclusive interest because reminders of more common emergencies, and how to cope with them, cannot be given too often.

Because of their nature and the terrain over which they run, motorways can be badly affected by extremes of weather. Chapter 8 therefore considers the problems that our climate poses for motorway driving.

In relation to their numbers, motorcyclists are not the most frequent users of motorways – perhaps because two-wheelers are primarily *fun* vehicles for many these days and even motorways' most ardent fans could hardly call them fun. One of the Institute's top motorcycle specialists, Rod Collins, has written Chapter 9 as a distillation of all his and his colleagues' motorway knowledge and experience.

Talking of knowledge and experience, no one could deny the amount of both gained by the IAM's team of examiners – the men and women who give you an hour and a half or so of very intensive testing in all sorts of driving conditions to see if you measure up to the Institute's strict standards. For Chapter 10, then, we have asked the team for hints and tips on motorway driving, and have made our selection of the best of them.

Finally, we equipped our Chief Examiner, Ted Clements, with a tape recorder and asked him to talk his way through his normal homeward run, in the late rush-hour, along the M4 and M25. His observations on and reactions to what is going on around him make fascinating reading.

2

THE MOTORWAY NETWORK

On the following pages we have set out the British motorway network as it exists at the time of publication. Largely, the system envisaged by the Government has been completed, although a number of links and gap-filling sections will appear before the end of the century.

In many instances, rather than construct a whole new motorway, existing trunk roads have been uprated bit by bit until they are virtually to motorway standard.

Take extra care on these, though, as they are still open to cyclists, and L-drivers can use them, thus gaining some early experience of what the real thing is going to be like once they pass the test.

Another hazard of these near-motorways is that they still have the occasional lane or even private drive turning off them at right angles, with all the attendant hazards when a vehicle joins or leaves the 70–80 mph stream.

Service areas

Motorway service areas have of course improved a great deal since the bad old days when many operators put service and quality well behind quick profits from a captive market. Most service area restaurants and cafeterias are very acceptable today to the vast majority of travellers.

Don't forget, though, that if you do not feel like pushing on to the next service area for fuel, food or just a rest – and it may, on some roads like the M25, be a long

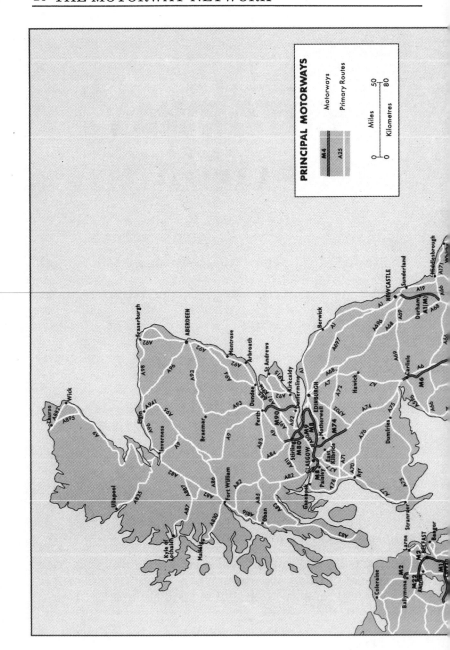

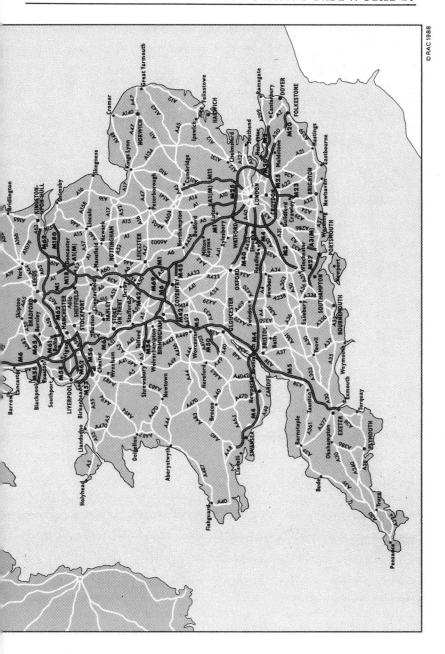

© RAC 1988

way before you get there – there is no reason not to break your journey at the next exit that is near a town of any size and seek sustenance there.

No excuse

Police were baffled when they saw a middle-eastern gentleman kneeling by his car on the hard shoulder of the M1. They were even more astonished when he said that he had pulled over – to pray. He told them 'I must pray five times a day so I stopped', but he was still fined £150 by Wakefield magistrates for halting illegally.

3

MOTORWAYS AND THE LAW

We all know – or think we know – the law as it applies to motorways:

> No stopping except in emergency
> No L-drivers, pedestrians, cyclists, horses or motorcycles under 50 cc
> Drive on the left except when overtaking
> Maximum speed 70 mph
> No heavy goods vehicles in the right-hand lane of 3-lane roads
> No U-turns

But is it that simple? As usual when the law is involved the answer is 'no', and it would take another book to expand on all the laws applying to motorway use and the way in which a solicitor, barrister or judge might interpret them.

All we can do is to reprint, by kind permission of Her

Motorway law is not as simple as many people think.

Majesty's Sationery Office, the Regulations as they apply at the time of publication to motorways in England, Scotland and Wales. They are printed in the appendix at the back of this book. We apologise to readers in Northern Ireland for not having the space to cover their own motorway law in such detail, and hope it will suffice to say that there are no significant differences from those applying elsewhere in the United Kingdom.

But before we go into the legalities, though, we should take a look at how some of the more important laws apply in detail and how the police enforce them.

Speed

Where the 70 mph limit is concerned, something of an anomaly exists. The Institute of Advanced Motorists, along with other motoring organisations, has been pressing for years for the maximum to be raised to 80 mph. The figure of 70 was introduced more than 20 years ago, when that was a reasonable maximum for many cars in view of the standards of roadholding, braking and steering of the day. Since then, cars have improved a great deal and the 70-limit looks and feels out of date to a majority of drivers. Today, 80 seems more realistic.

Most of Britain's senior police officers agree with this sentiment, but even they have been unable to convince the Government that a change is needed.

Many drivers try to maintain a steady 70 mph where conditions permit. But do they know how accurate their speedometers are? New car speedos are allowed by law to be anything up to 10 per cent fast, so most manufacturers aim at having instruments around 5 per cent optimistic. This means that at a true 70 mph your speedometer may be showing anything between 70 and 77 mph – probably around 74 mph – and that's quite a range of error. Older car speedometers, could be between 10 per cent fast and 10 per cent slow. Bear in mind too, that the police make allowance for speedo error in cars.

You can check your own speedo, with the help of a passenger, next time you are on a fairly empty motorway. Observing the marker posts to the left of the hard shoulder which are spaced every tenth of a kilometre, drive for 4 km

– about 2½ miles – with a steady 70 mph on the speedo and time how long it takes. The following table shows times and true speeds for the 4 kms.

Seconds:	150	145	140	135	130	128.5	125	120
MPH:	60	62	64.3	66.7	69.2	70	72	75

Remember, though, that *some* speedos – maybe yours – are dead accurate.

Motorway speed limits are more complex than they seem, since the 70-limit is not an overall one and some categories of vehicles are restricted to 60 mph. Briefly, the position is as follows:

70 mph: cars, motorcycles, dual purpose vehicles – such as small motor caravans as defined in Reg. 3 Road Vehicles (Construction and Use) Regulations 1986, car-derived vans, motor caravans, coaches adapted to carry more than eight passengers but under 12 metres in length or with an unladen weight exceeding 3.05 tonnes, and trucks and vans with a maximum laden weight not exceeding 7.5 tonnes – provided they are not articulated and not towing a trailer.

60 mph: any vehicle towing a trailer, be it a caravan, boat trailer or similar right up to an artic unit, and goods vehicles with a maximum laden weight of over 7.5 tonnes.

We also look forward to the day when a minimum speed limit is introduced. Slow moving vehicles on busy motorways constitute a mobile hazard, with traffic stacking up behind and then becoming caught in dangerous lane-changing manoeuvres as impeded drivers seek to move out into the centre lane traffic to overtake.

Lanes

Moving on to lane usage, this is an aspect of motorway law on which successive Governments have failed to grasp the nettle of re-defining the rules. Clearly, on all but the quietest motorway it is no more than a pious hope to expect traffic to keep to the left-hand lane except when overtaking. The occasional pedant who does so, while travelling at 70 mph or more, creates untold hazards as he darts across one or two more lanes, then scurries back to the left-hand lane for a brief pause before swerving out to overtake again. Most drivers finish up – more or less illegally – sticking to whichever line of traffic, in whichever lane, best suits their cruising speed. As motorways become more and more heavily used, this custom is increasingly the norm and the time may not be far off when the Department of Transport has to take a long, hard look at just how many motorway lanes are properly used in reality. If nothing else, some re-defining of the law may increase lane utilisation but as things stand, there is definite room for improvement.

No one seems very clear even over what to call each lane. Common usage refers to 'slow', 'middle' and 'fast' lanes and however right this might be in practice it is certainly wrong in theory. Most police forces prefer to number them, 1, 2 and 3, adding clockwise/anti-clockwise for good measure when it comes to the M25 encircling London. In the IAM's view, left-hand, middle and right-hand lanes are the safest description. For a four-lane motorway, the Department of Transport suggests nearside, nearside centre, outside centre and outside.

Warning signs

One day we may have an efficient system of motorway signalling. As traffic volume and speed increase year by year it is certainly needed, to alert drivers to problems

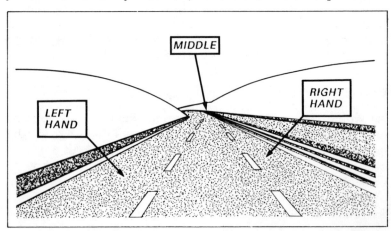

ahead, give them the chance to slow early or even leave the motorway at the next junction, or keep down to a reduced speed.

As things stand, most motorway mileage is effectively unsignalled, and where signals do exist they often seem to be switched on too late, or left on long after the hazard has abated so that drivers treat them with scant regard.

The light signal system is simple enough, with the Lane Ahead Closed being obvious, when a vertical bar with a T-barred top, next to unbarred verticals, shows. The speed limits which occasionally flash up are advisory. The rectangle crossed by a diagonal signifies All Clear. At all major roadworks and contra-flow systems mandatory speed limits have now been introduced.

Motorway repairs

Compared to their Continental and American counterparts British motorways seem to be in a constant state of repair. The prime reason is that in planning the majority of them, the Government of the day has opted for quantity rather than quality, trading the savings of shallow foundations for extra route mileage.

Now that traffic volumes are higher than have been forecast, wear is made worse by the pounding process of trucks heavier than those envisaged a few years ago.

However, things may improve one day. For example, once the over-trafficked south-west sector of the M25 gets its fourth lanes, the old road will be dug up and replaced by a newer one of higher specification and a 'life' of 20 years. We can only hope that this policy will be repeated for all motorway rebuilds.

Another possibility is that the number of apparently pointlessly coned-off lanes will be reduced. This follows a decision to denote 'mobile' road works such as white-lining and weed-spraying, by mounting 'Lane Closure' and other signs at the rear of special vehicles moving in convoy along the hard shoulder. But beware, these slow convoys will themselves present a hazard as traffic slows to shuffle across into the middle and outer lanes to avoid them.

Mandatory speed limits under these circumstances have been imposed on a semi-experimental basis by a few

Cones are still used extensively to mark roadworks.

police forces since 1984, but there are considerable difficulties in enforcing them.

What a bore

Drivers once had to swerve to avoid a hole-boring machine which burst up through the nearside lane of the M1. The automatic drill, boring a tunnel under the motorway for cables, made a 2ft-wide hole in the northbound carriageway. A police spokesman said 'It gave us a very busy time and could have caused a nasty accident. We were very lucky!'

4

ADVANCED DRIVING

Just as on any ordinay road, the techniques of advanced driving are essential for the motorway.

The basis is a planned, systematic – yet not rigid – approach to conducting a vehicle on the road. It also entails a 'thinking', and non-aggressive approach: it's as important to de-fuse the potential accident situations that other people inadvertently create as to avoid setting up possible hazards by one's own bad driving.

On the motorway the main points to remember are these:

Observation

Even more than on other roads, because of the higher speeds involved and the inadequate braking distances many drivers allow themselves, you must look well ahead. Just concentrating on the vehicle immediately in front in a

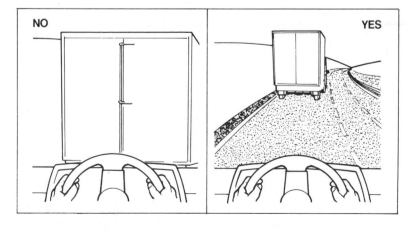

close packed line of traffic moving at 70 or more mph is not enough. By hanging well back (and thus keeping that all important thinking-then-braking distance) you will be able to see further down the line, looking through the rear windows and windscreens of cars ahead where it helps.

Thus when brake lights do go on, or any other hazard starts to evolve up ahead, you have ample warning.

Similarly, you must *give* ample warning when considering a change of pace or direction of your own. Check the mirrors, and glance to either side, for observation is a 360-degree operation. By keeping a watchful eye in this way, an advanced driver will at any time be aware of the nature and proximity of the traffic around him on the motorway.

Planning, tolerance

Many motorway accidents are caused by last-second decisions to change lanes or take a fast approaching exit road. Plan each move well in advance, so that before you start to alter course you know where your vehicle neighbours are and the speed you need to hold the vehicle at to make the manoeuvre safely and avoid inconveniencing anyone else.

The Institute of Advanced Motorists has a memory jogger for the sequence of events needed for changes of course or direction: Can My Safety Be Given Away? The initial letters represent:

Course – plan it early
Mirror – check behind, and to the sides
Signal – give the indicator signal early, and well before you
  start the manoeuvre
Brake – unlikely to be necessary on the motorway, except
  in emergency, as simple deceleration will usually ease
  your speed down sufficiently
Gear – especially in cars with a high–ratio 'economy' fifth
  for cruising you may well need to come down a gear to
  have enough acceleration in hand should the situation
  suddenly warrant it
Acceleration – if all the above operations have been
  carried out then is the time to start the manoeuvre itself.

Motorways, especially those in urban areas, are notorious as the motoring playground of those with driving psychoses of one kind or another to work off. The car, truck or coach driver who keeps his front bumper six inches from yours while you are both in a line of fast moving traffic, perhaps even flashing his lights, clearly has a desperate need to assert himself. By forcing past you in the 70 mph queue he is not going to reach his destination more than a few seconds sooner. It's best to let him through, simply because you do not want such a fool so close to your vehicle. The rule is Keep Calm, Don't Retaliate.

Similarly, the driver who carves you up with what seems like a deliberate swerve into your lane is best ignored. Don't fight back.

There are, on the other hand, many opportunities on the motorway for courtesy to play a part. Notably, easing back to let joining traffic in at a junction – and, better still, moving to the centre or right-hand lane as you approach

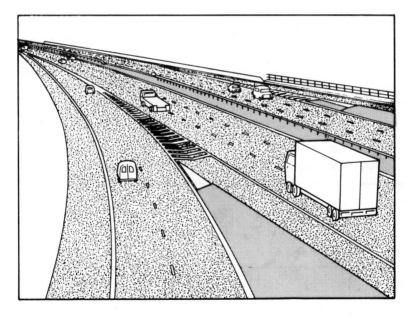

that junction so as to leave the left-hand one clear for them. Make sure, though, that by doing so you are not holding up anyone else.

Another reason to move out into the centre lane is that in the rush hour in urban areas the left-hand lane will quickly fill with a tailback of traffic queueing at the next exit. Then even more drivers form a second line, which also tails back and soon fills more of the left-hand and even middle lane back on the motorway itself.

If you are not already a member of the IAM you may like to consider taking the Institute's advanced test, which is detailed elsewhere in this book. The IAM was founded in 1956 as a non-profit-making road safety charity, dedicated to reducing the accident rate by improving driving standards. From a network of locations covering the whole of the United Kingdom it provides an advanced test for drivers of cars, commercial vehicles, buses and coaches and for riders of motorcycles above 200 cc. All examiners are retired or serving police officers with the Police Class One certificate needed for traffic patrol work, generally accepted as the highest driving 'award' in Britain. To help candidates prepare for the test, the Institute has more than 180 area associations of members, known as Groups, most of which will provide advanced driving guidance and advice on a voluntary basis to prospective candidates.

At headquarters the Institute has a Fleet Training operation which offers a range of tuition services for company vehicle drivers (see Chapter 15 for more details).

To find out more about the advanced test, to obtain a test application form, or to discuss Fleet Training contact the Institute at IAM House, 359 Chiswick High Road, London W4 4HS or by phoning 01-994 4403. There are also application forms and full details of the advanced test at the end of this book.

Starting young

Some years back, police who approached a car that had run out of petrol on the M5 near Worcester found the driver was a boy of 12. He had driven on the motorway for 27 miles.

5

JOINING AND LEAVING THE MOTORWAY

Many motorway approach roads run down from elevated roundabouts, giving you a reasonable opportunity to check the traffic on the main carriageway as you prepare to filter into it. Even before you turn into the slip-road itself, though, take a preliminary look at the 'state of play'; this is especially worthwhile should bad weather, heavy rush-hour traffic or an accident be causing a blockage farther on.

If, while still on the roundabout, you can see that the traffic on the motorway is stationary or moving very slowly, you still have time to take your chance on ordinary roads. However, once you are properly on the slip-road, beyond the motorway sign, you have passed the point of

The narrow, climbing slip road where the A4 joins the M4.

no return. If you change your mind *never* reverse up the slip-road; you are committing a serious traffic offence. Although the Highway Code advises that, if there is not a suitable gap in the traffic in the left-hand lane, you may wait in the accelerating lane, the skilled driver will always try to adjust speed while in the acceleration lane to join the motorway smoothly without changing speed unduly.

Should your preliminary survey indicate that the road is reasonably clear, you can safely drive down the slip-road, glancing on your right to assess the vehicle situation astern as well as observing what is ahead. Resist the temptation to overtake any but the slowest 'heavy' on the slip-road even if, as is usual, it has two lanes; injudicious passing on the run down could leave you travelling too fast for a smooth and unobstructive entry to the motorway itself, and with a disconcerted or annoyed driver in your wake. It doesn't make sense just to save a few seconds on your journey time.

Some slip-roads are split where they feed into the motorway to give two distinct paths of approach, with the order 'Stay in lane' and a clearly marked do-not-enter hatched area between them. The separation of the lanes (as they must reach the through carriageway of the motorway) is to ensure that the traffic joining the motorway does so one lane at a time. This enables much safer merging of the joining traffic with that already on the motorway. The reason is not just to increase the capacity of the junction as a whole but, and more importantly, substantially to increase the safety of the junction and those using the slip-road on the motorway.

These divisions double the number of vehicles that can be on the slip-road at once, and they work well enough as long as drivers choose their lane at the outset and stick to it until actually on the main carriageway. So if you encounter one of these two-stream slip-roads, treat it normally and stick to the inside lane unless this is already full.

Do your best to keep clear of other joining traffic as you plan your move out into the carriageway. You will be busy enough getting ready to deal with heavy main-carriageway streams without the distractions of other vehicles immediately ahead of or alongside you on the slip-road.

M3/M25 junction. Drivers must know well in advance whether they are to travel clockwise or anti-clockwise.

Cats eyes – or reflecting studs – are white to mark the lanes, red to mark the left edge of the carriageway, amber to mark the right edge, near the central reservation and green to show entries and exits from slip roads.

Tucking yourself in

As you approach the main carriageway, accelerate up to what you judge is the speed of any traffic coming up in the inner lane, your objective being to slip into place without a sudden last moment change of pace. Pick your gap early, aiming of course for one of ample length, and start signalling early too; a 'right-turn' signal may seem indicating the obvious, but it does awaken any dozy drivers already on the motorway to the fact that they are about to have company.

Although your joining speed should be synchronised with that of left-hand-lane traffic, avoid accelerating so hard that you become guilty of overtaking on the inside.

Most important as you cover the last stretch of the slip-road: don't dither! You *have* to find a gap and move into it, and your chances of doing so are greatest when you are travelling at the same speed as the stream in the left-hand lane. To slow to a crawl or even have to stop because you have reached the end of the slip-road without 'getting in' is not merely ignominious but downright dangerous. Those behind will now have to pull out around the obstruction *you* have created, while drivers on the motorway itself are faced with slow moving traffic on their left and so may have to swerve into the middle lane to avoid it. And you are just as much at risk, being still faced with the problem of getting in – and now with the added hazard of a standing start and a big speed differential.

Whatever gap you choose, enter it firmly and decisively, but not forcefully – sometimes quite a fine distinction. Leave as much braking distance as possible for the driver behind you, and adjust your speed to his as soon

When joining a motorway, select a gap in the traffic on the left-hand lane and adjust your speed to suit it.

as you are in the lane, so that he is not inconvenienced.

If the motorway driver behind gives you a flash of the headlights as you are about to emerge, treat it only as a 'Look out; don't forget I'm here' warning of his presence, not as an invitation to slot in. People can mean different things by such a flash, so for safety's sake always take the pessimistic view.

Having got into the left-hand lane, stay there for a few seconds before venturing out into the next lane should you wish to overtake; if you don't, stay where you are and leave the other two lanes to the faster traffic. An entry that brings you belting down the slip-road, out into the left-hand lane and then immediately over to the middle lane or even the right-hand one could be fatal. Making a safe transition into that inner lane is often hard enough in itself without your adding to the hazard by pulling out – probably unsighted owing to left-hand traffic astern– into the middle and right-hand streams.

Other approaches

So far, we have dealt only with joining a motorway via a descending slip-road – the easiest approach of all. Where the entry is 'on the level', much the same rules apply but with the important difference that you will not have such a good view of the traffic already on the motorway. The only safe technique is to pay even more attention to what is already out there during your few seconds on the slip-road. Sizing up the speed-and-distance situation for the other vehicles in your vicinity and aiming for the right gap at the right speed clearly demand your full concentration.

By far the hardest motorways to join are the urban ones. This is not just because the traffic is often very dense and fast-moving or even because the reasonable manners of 'out in the country' motorway driving tend to be replaced as one reaches a major city by selfishness and aggression. Rather is it endemic to the urban pattern.

A classic example, barely a mile from the IAM office, is where the old A4 Great West Road is linked to the M4, running there on a viaduct. Short ramp roads lead steeply up to the motorway which has frighteningly narrow two-lane carriageways with no hard shoulders and is hemmed-in with Armco barrier like the Monaco Grand Prix circuit – a monument to the dangers of cheese-paring in road building.

On account of the very impaired view, the joining driver has but a fraction of the usual time in which to assess the traffic he must filter into, and only a brief stretch in which to accelerate up to the joining speed – and to make his/her entry. The special technique? There's none; only decisiveness, quick reactions and sound judgement in allowing for a safe gap. The only saving grace of this particular situation is that it proved sufficiently lethal for a 50 mph limit to be imposed.

There is no doubt that, not only on urban motorways such as this but also at busy interchanges outside the cities, present entry points are often inadequate for rush-hour traffic volumes. Understandably to some extent, successive Governments shrink from spending millions to cure a problem which exists for only a few hours a day, five days a week. But the problem is worsening, causing more hold-ups where sliproads meet motorways, plus tailbacks or blocking the feeder roads.

A possible solution, not yet much favoured in Britain but working well enough abroad, is to install peak-hours-only traffic lights at the start of slip-roads. These are phased to allow only a few vehicles at a time on to the slip-road, so they at least have a clear run for their acceleration. The jam still builds up but back along the feeder road – not so far back, at that, because of the clearer entry on to the motorway.

A final point of advice to those joining motorways is to remember what police motorcyclists call 'the lifesaver' – a quick glance back over your right shoulder to see that the coast really is clear. Even the best mirror systems, internal or on door or wing, can leave dangerous blind-spots encompassing other and fast-moving vehicles.

The hazard may be reduced but not completely eliminated by a blind-spot mirror (usually with a convex surface to widen the field of view) stuck on the driver's outside mirror. But that backward glance over the shoulder is still the best. Make it quick, though, since in

those particular conditions you cannot afford to have your
eyes off the road ahead for long.

Getting off again

So much for joining a motorway. Leaving it is a less fraught
business but still needs care and a planned, systematic and
decisive approach.

Stage 1, as always in advanced driving, is planning.
Know well in advance what you are going to do and when
you will have to do it – something that goes all the way
back to preparing for the journey itself. Find out from the
map where you will be leaving the motorway, so that you
know the junction number and what to expect on the signs.
The number is the more critical information since those
responsible for the signing of motorways are sometimes
confusing in their efforts to be helpful.

*When leaving or changing motorways, get in the correct lane in good time
– at the very latest by the 300-yard marker.*

Let us assume you have been in the West Country and are intending to leave the northbound M5 for Taunton. You will probably do the obvious thing and peel off at the exit marked Taunton, but you will be wrong. The first Taunton exit is in fact well to the south and, although you can eventually get to that town via meandering country roads, the exit's main purpose is to serve various villages. You *should* have stuck to the M5 as far as a later junction which, also signed Taunton, will get you there much more quickly and directly.

So, with the correct exit point firmly in mind, start looking out for it early. It's all too easy to miss that departure point through inattention or because a truck in the left-hand lane obscures your view of the sign.

If you are in the middle or right-hand lane, begin moving over well in advance, to ensure being in the left-hand lane in good time for the exit. The last-second plunge across from the outside, cutting a swathe through the other traffic, is potentially very, very dangerous.

Your final warning of the junction is the three marker boards. These carry oblique bars – three indicating that you are 300 yards from the start of the slip-road, two for 200 yards and one for 100 yards. They can help you adjust your speed accurately for an easy divergence into the slip-road. Check your mirrors as you approach the first marker board. At this point signal a left turn and, if necessary, reduce speed in preparation for entering the slip-road. If traffic is heavy, begin the move earlier. Do not dart across other traffic from the middle.

Another point to watch on leaving the motorway is that not everyone leaves at the start of the slip-road. Some tend to make the turn late and will unthinkingly cut across anyone already on the slip-road.

If you miss the exit altogether do not even think of reversing along the hard shoulder. It is illegal and very dangerous. Resign yourself to going on to the next junction. Believe it or not, people do attempt it – and worse. There are cases on record of drivers who, overshooting the exit, have simply turned round and headed back, in the right-hand lane of the same carriageway. And, quite recently, drivers finding their side of the M2 blocked by snow changed carriageway at a gap in the central reservation and pressed on along the other half of the motorway. Always remember: there are dangerous fools out there and, since they are unlikely to change, it's up to the rest of us to avoid them.

Still with an eye astern for anyone following you too closely, ease your speed further to be ready for the end of the slip-road. A few exit slips lead out straight on to main roads where the white-lining may give you priority, but someone may not be obeying the rules so be ready for an emergency stop. However, most slips lead up to roundabouts where, even if a queue has not built up, you will almost certainly have to slow down or even stop.

Here we come to a critical aspect of motorway driving. You may well have been driving at 70 mph for some time. Your senses, in particular your judgement of speed, have become adapted to that and are heightened by the motorway's wide open spaces and relative featurelessness. Suddenly you are on a narrow slip-road heading possibly for a stop only a short distance away and moving at a pace is still very fast. The roundabout ahead is coming up much faster than you expected, so your brakes – hardly touched for many miles – are needed *now* for a panic stop which, with proper planning would never have been necessary.

We end this chapter, therefore, with a word of warning: when leaving a motorway, never forget that your judgement of speed is bound to be temporarily impaired. The moral is to slow down – yes, really slow down – early on the slip-road to a sensible speed (according to your speedometer, not your senses), for *anything* that may be coming up ahead. And don't put your caution on one side when you pull away from that roundabout at the end of the slip-road; it's going to take you several miles to readjust to the more leisurely pace (and speed limits down to 30 mph) of the ordinary road system.

Madness

The myriad forms of 'motorway madness' include people who pray, stroll, shave at the wheel or become locked in passionate embraces at 70 mph. They walk on the motorway to clear obstructions or dart across all six lanes to reach an emergency telephone on the hard shoulder opposite. Children roll down steep banks of cuttings straight on to the M1 and challenge each other to games of 'last across'. Those who pray are usually Moslems. An Arab who explained to the motorway police that he was praying towards Mecca was told: 'You're pointing the wrong way; the Mecca service station is to the north of here.'

6

ON THE MOTORWAY

All the tenets of good driving behaviour on ordinary roads apply also on motorways, but some of them are of especially high significance because of particular characteristics – notably the generally higher speeds. No better starting point could be found for this chapter than the slogan See And Be Seen, because without these dual abilities no one has a chance of driving safely on a motorway.

See and be seen

On the **see** side, clean glass is essential, so be generous with the screen-washer liquid in dirty conditions; don't try to eke it out until you get home because you can always refill the reservoir at the next service garage – usually for nothing. If you are travelling at night and have a car without a headlamp wash/wipe, use each stop to clean those lenses. Even a thin film of road dirt on the glass can cut the light output by 30 per cent or more, and that could make all the difference between seeing an obstacle in time or too late.

A clean inside to the glazing is important as well so, apart from regular cleansing treatment, avoid misting-up on the journey by sensible use of the ventilation system and the glass-heating element(s). Cars are often seen on motorways with extensively misted glass, so make sure you are not yet another unseeing offender.

As to **being seen**, remember that you are not going to prolong the life of your battery by not turning on your lights when darkness is falling or the weather deteriorates.

More is said about driving in fog and rain in Chapter 7 but a point is worth making here about the use of high-intensity rear lamps. These can be a great safety benefit when spray or fog cut down the visibility, but the Law is quite clear that they must *not* be used except in such circumstances on account of the dazzle hazard to following drivers. The Highway Code says front low-mounted auxiliary lamps are legal only in fog or falling snow, under the same conditions.

Awareness

The higher speeds mentioned earlier mean that things tend to happen more quickly than on ordinary roads, so the safe driver has to make the appropriate adjustments to his technique. To avoid being the *cause* of an incident, he or she has to keep the eyes peeled in all directions – ahead, astern and to the sides – so as to know what all the immediately surrounding vehicles are doing, and give generous warning of any intention to overtake by changing lanes or to leave the motorway, as covered in the previous chapter.

All too frequently, drivers are surprised by slower cars suddenly pulling out into their path to pass yet slower vehicles. If they were reading the road properly, in the best IAM manner, they would have known from the relative speeds that a passing manoeuvre was imminent and would have been ready to take the appropriate action. Nevertheless, it is up to the first overtaker to give lots of warning, and that implies thorough and frequent use of the mirrors.

Close-to awareness is only part of the picture, of course. One should also be looking well ahead for other people's incidents or accidents-in-the-making, in which one could become involved through lack of anticipation. It is hardly necessary to point out that the best early warning of 'something happening up front' is a sudden firework display of brake lights, but one should also be looking out constantly for warning road signs.

This practice of reading the road, looking well ahead for the telltale warning signs that keep you prepared for any developing hazard, is crucial to safe motorway travel.

Too many drivers drive too close behind other vehicles.

Lack of concentration and failure to plan ahead are major causes of motorway accidents. Your observation, when visibility allows, should be for a mile or more ahead. That way, you have the maximum time in which to prepare for whatever hazards are building up.

One early warning sign to watch for is when the gap between vehicles ahead starts to close. Clearly someone up front is slowing down.

It is usually facilitated by the fact that many motorways have been built as a series of long and gentle curves, undulating across the landscape. This is partly for aesthetic reasons – they simply look better that way and harmonise more with their natural surroundings. But such a format also helps keep drivers more alert and enables a weather eye to be kept on traffic well ahead by affording a better view – even if it is often slightly above or to one side of the vehicles in front.

However, some of our early motorways and others that traverse very flat terrain, contain long stretches of dead straight road where visibility is much more impeded by the traffic up ahead. The answer is to hang back even further.

Lane discipline

Those who drive extensively on the European mainland are well aware how inferior motorway lane discipline is in the UK compared with over there. The biggest single sin of British car drivers is to 'hog' the middle lane of a motorway when the left-hand lane is empty, or the right-hand lane when there is nothing in the middle one for some distance ahead.

This behaviour is partly laziness/doziness but it is also indication of unqualified ignorance or selfishness. By driving in the middle lane when the left-hand one is clear, a driver is, in effect, occupying *two* lanes to those approaching from astern, since in Britain they are not normally allowed to pass you on the left. The HGV driver is even worse off because *he* may not be allowed to pass you on the right either, so in effect you are taking up his entire road. We know too that those hogging the right-hand lane are usually in the over-70 mph category, but even so they are occupying all of everyone else's road.

It is up to everyone, but particularly perhaps those who drive to the advanced standard of the IAM, to set an example here by making maximum use of lanes to facilitate traffic flow while adhering to the law.

Encountering both types of selfish drivers, as one does for instance on any trip on the M1, makes one wonder whether our law should not be amended to allow 'discretionary' passing on the nearside of the middle and outer lanes. Normally, you should never overtake on the left, but where the traffic is moving in queues, and the traffic queue on your right is going more slowly than you are, you may maintain the speed of the traffic in your own lane and so pass on the left.

Reverting to 'lane hogging', though, the general principle should be that one keeps in the left-hand lane. However, if one is driving at 70 mph in traffic, it may be sensible in *practice* to hold the middle-lane position continuously, simply to avoid relatively frequent movements outward and inward again. This only applies in conditions of medium and dense traffic. If you follow this precept, you must of course keep an eye in the mirror all the time so as to be ready to move over if someone comes up astern.

When moving into the middle lane from either the left-hand or right-hand lanes it is not enough just to check that the middle one is clear. Ensure also that no one is about to change lane at the same time, aiming for the same spot in the middle as you have in mind, from the opposite

Lorry drivers must comply with different rules and limits.

lane (that is, the left-hand if you are in the right-hand, and vice versa).

Some work on a time basis. If they are just passing someone, in the middle lane, and estimate that at least ten seconds will elapse before they reach the next vehicle in the inside lane, then they pull over; otherwise they stay out.

The repetition of useful information never does any harm, so think about this one. When you are about to overtake and signal accordingly, you are showing *only* an intention to change lanes. The signal does not entitle you to move out regardless of other traffic. No one, least of all IAM members, has any divine right to change lanes – an activity that is proably one of the most potentially dangerous on the motorway. The other side of this particular motorway coin is the 'holier than thou', spot-on-70 driver who refuses to move from the outside lane when a faster driver comes up, on the ground that he is preventing the other from breaking the law. Get out of the way and let the speedster do his 90 if he wants. After all, *he* pays the fine.

Braking distances

Higher speeds on motorways than ordinary roads have a direct relationship to the braking distances that can be achieved in an emergency. More accurately it is a 'square' relationship in that those distances increase as the square of the speed – ie twice the speed means four times the

SHORTEST STOPPING DISTANCES – IN FEET			
MPH	THINKING DISTANCE	BRAKING DISTANCE	OVERALL STOPPING DISTANCE
20	20	20	40
30	30	45	75
40	40	80	120
50	50	125	175
60	60	180	240
70	70	245	315
80	80	320	400

braking distance. Because of this square law it is very easy to under-estimate how far a vehicle will travel under heavy braking before it comes to rest.

The accompanying table of stopping distances from various speeds are for a car with good brakes on a dry road and include what is commonly called the 'thinking distance' – how far the vehicle goes between the driver's awareness of the need for an emergency stop and actually getting the brakes on. The higher the speed, clearly, the greater the thinking distance, and older drivers should not forget that their reactions are almost certainly slower than when they were 20 or 30.

This table, based on figures given in the Highway Code, shows the braking performance of a car with good brakes and tyres and with an alert driver. These are the shortest stopping distances and they increase greatly in wet and slippery conditions, with poor brakes and tyres – and a tired driver.

It is also important to remember that on approaching any line of stationary traffic, such as that which occurs when a vehicle breaks down in a contraflow system, the situation is made worse by the fact that such a blockage is *not* actually stationary. It is building 'backards' at the rate of many miles per hour as more vehicles tail on to the end. This further reduces braking distance.

Heavy commercial vehicles, buses and coaches have lower ultimate deceleration rates than cars and motorbikes. They are much heavier yet still only have that slender footprint of rubber keeping them in contact with the road. Always take a quick look in the mirror if you have to brake sharply on a motorway; better to digress briefly on to the hard shoulder than have a truck in the boot.

Another early warning signal of the need to slow down is that cars up ahead under heavy braking will dip their noses and lift their tails – whereas light braking will leave their trim undisturbed. It's little signs like these that give you valuable extra time to start your own braking.

Awareness of braking distances becomes especially relevant if another driver nips past you on a crowded stretch – commonly on the run into a contraflow or under-repair section where the number of lanes is temporarily reduced – and makes to cut in. It is very tempting sometimes to 'protect your domain', accelerating to shut the offender out, but this is something you should never do on a motorway although in theory it is less dangerous than on a single-carriageway road where you may push the pusher into a head-on collision. The greater risk on the motorway is that in accelerating you will reduce your own braking distance to a hazardous extent. So be patient and philosophical.

Maintain the braking distance you need at all costs, even if someone moves over into your lane and occupies some of it. Do not retaliate, stay cool and drop back to keep that all important space. It should be at least in line with the 'two second rule' favoured by the police and the Department of Transport. Allow a gap which keeps you a minimum of two seconds behind the next vehicle – roughly the time it takes to say 'one second, two seconds', taking some roadside sign as a marker. (Even two seconds is not much; at 70 mph it's only 205 feet).

Other points

A complementary cause of concern on motorways is the 'tailgater' – the driver who persists in driving so close behind that he is bound to shunt you if you have to brake hard in an emergency. He is very difficult to deal with. You can try accelerating but the chances are that he will speed up with you and you will end up exceeding 70 mph or going faster than your comfortable cruising gait.

You should certainly not dab the brakes in the hope of frightening him off, because unless he is wide awake he could collide with the rear of your vehicle. Sometimes going slower and slower does the trick because he gets bored with his poor progress, but here you have to be careful to avoid becoming a hazard yourself by dropping below the speed of the other traffic in your lane.

If you and your tormentor have been in the middle lane, you can try switching, at a convenient moment, to the inside one – maybe he will not fancy having nothing but hard shoulder on his left.

One of the hazards one encounters on motorways, because some of the gradients are very long, is the 'mobile chicane' of a line of slow-moving heavy trucks on an ascent. On some roads, such as the M6, a so-called crawler lane is provided – a great help to faster traffic. Where there are only two or three lanes, though, one should always be ready for one of the more powerful trucks (or more impatient drivers) to pull out to overtake. If it succeeds at all, the operation is going to take quite a lot of time and distance to complete, so you should be ready for quick acceleration to take you past him – or for a spell in which to practise patient driving.

7

EMERGENCIES ON THE MOTORWAY

The safety-conscious driver will certainly not want to *cause* an emergency of any kind, and one way to 'stay clean' is to make sure that the vehicle is properly maintained and in good working order.

Very little time and trouble are entailed before a motorway journey in checking oil and water levels, and in making sure that the tank contains at least enough fuel to reach the first service area. To have your engine fail or boil, or to run out of fuel, while motoring at 70 mph in the right-hand lane is a certain recipe for an emergency – and one that could involve a lot of other vehicles and people.

Tyre check

At least as important as levels are your tyres – your only areas of contact with the road. Tyre bursts are not uncommon on motorways – *vide* the number of shed treads from trucks that one sees – and in most cases they are the result of under-inflation. A soft tyre, as its elements move on to and off the road surface, flexes more than a correctly inflated one, and excessive flexing generates heat which is the arch-enemy of the rubber and fabric used in the tyre's construction. The higher the speed (as on a motorway), the greater the flexing frequency, and hence the heat generation and risk of failure. Remember that a burst tyre can cause loss of steering control.

An under-inflated tyre will overheat and could even

Tyre failures are a common cause of breakdown on motorways.

disintegrate. Check your owners' manual to see whether a higher pressure is recommended for protracted motorway use – although bear in mind that your speed should not be over 70 mph so may not be high enough to necessitate extra pressure. If you do raise pressures remember to lower them again later – and remember that meaningful tyre pressures are only available with the tyres cold.

So, if more than a couple of weeks have elapsed since the last time, get out the tyre gauge and check pressures all round. At the same time have a look round the tyres for sharp embedded objects or suspicious bulges in the sidewalls. Such bulges, usually the result of driving up kerbs at other than a crawl, are unlikely to cause trouble around town but they do indicate a seriously weakened tyre carcase which, of course, is more likely to fail in the arduous conditions of motorway driving.

If a tyre punctures – or more alarmingly, bursts – the rules are: **1** Keep calm. **2** Do not brake hard or swerve over to the hard shoulder. **3** Steer gently across and brake lightly if necessary. Just as when driving on ice, only harsh use of the controls will provoke a skid.

Motorway drowsiness

On the theme of personal responsibility, let's consider the sleepiness that affects a surprisingly large number of drivers on the motorway. It has various causes, such as straightforward tiredness at the ned of a long day, boredom, a large meal, drink, even if consumed quite a while ago, and some medicines. (Not *just* the anti-histamines used to counter allergies such as hay fever.)

However induced, drowsiness tends to creep up on you and sap your awareness, to the extent that you do not realise something needs to be done. You have to make yourself face up to the possibility of drowsiness before you get on to the motorway, to establish a suitably precautionary attitude of mind. Then, immediately you become aware of the first symptom – maybe a heavy feeling of the eyelids or the tendency of your gaze to become fixed – **take action**.

Drowsiness does not constitute an emergency, so you should not pull off on to the hard shoulder. Your target should be the first exit, whether junction or service area. In the meantime open the windows wide and breathe deeply of the good fresh air. And, if you have a passenger, get him/her to chat with you (not just talk *to* you). The radio is at least a reasonable alternative.

When you get off the motorway and can stop safely and legally, there are several things you can do to fight off the dreaded torpor. Some people find it sufficient just to run down the road and back for 100 yards or so (or even 'on the spot'), to get the lungs doing a bit of work and thus stir the circulation. If you have pulled into a service area a

Do not be distracted by unusual happenings on the motorway.

brisk walk over to the restaurant and a cup of tea or coffee are bound to improve matters. Or maybe you are one of those who must get their heads down – as short a nap as ten minutes is often enough.

The hard shoulder

In the event of a vehicle failure of any kind, you *must* get over to the hard shoulder quickly, if you possibly can. That, incidentally, is an additional reason for driving in as leftward a lane as you can – it isn't so far to the shoulder. Even with a burst tyre you have to struggle across at the risk of damaging cover and rim. That short distance could be yet more of an obstacle if the engine has failed, but don't forget that you may be able to cover the last few

While awaiting help, seek the safety of a grass verge or bank.

yards on the starter motor, with the car in bottom gear.

When you come to rest on the hard shoulder, the first thing to do is switch on the hazard flashers as a warning to other vehicles to keep clear. Even so, you could be better off out of the car and on the grass where possible because it is by no means unknown for stopped vehicles to be hit by others driven too close to the edge of the carriageway. If you carry a red warning triangle, as we recommend, set it up 150 metres back along the hard shoulder. Don't forget it when you get going again. When you move off to rejoin the traffic stream use the hard shoulder to gain the necessary joining speed.

If the cause of the stoppage is a burst tyre or a puncture, changing a wheel on the hard shoulder is not a pleasant task, especially on the offside where the traffic thunders past terrifyingly close. In that case there is nothing craven in summoning assistance via the nearest emergency telephone and letting the professional breakdown man do the work, using his bigger and more conspicuous vehicle as a shield. The little arrows on the 100 metre posts indicate which way to the nearest 'phone, and you do *not* have to be a member of one of the motoring organisations to use them.

If you are on the hard shoulder awaiting help, stay out of your vehicle and some distance to its left – eg on the bank. Unless the weather is really cold or foul, this will be pleasanter as well as safer than sitting in the car only a few feet from the traffic. Don't overdo the leftward bias, though, or you may find yourself in soft soil or a ditch, or falling down an embankment. If you break down on a bridge or flyover where there is no verge or hard shoulder, stay in your vehicle.

Supposing, unlikely though it is, you should be unfortunate enough to get stranded by a breakdown *on the carriageway*, with no means of driving to the hard shoulder – what then? First switch on hazard warning lights and high-intensity rear lights for additional visibility. If you are able-bodied and consider that you can get to the hard shoulder on foot, do realise that a car travelling at 70 mph is covering 35 yards per second. Then get to the nearest emergency telephone and report the obstruction.

Other emergencies and tips

So far we have been discussing emergencies in which you might have been involved, so let's now turn to the other category – those happening to other people. This at once brings us to the secondary use of hazard flashers, as a moving warning to following vehicles. If the brake lights suddenly come on everywhere up front (indicating the likelihood of a quick stoppage), or you encounter an unexpected bank of fog, and there is traffic behind you, it makes good sense to give those astern as much advance warning as possible by switching your hazard warning lights. The use of hazard warning lights on motorways is to be permitted to warn following drivers of a need to slow down due to a temporary obstruction ahead.

Prior warning

Forewarned is forearmed so it pays to listen to local and national radio news programmes which are often followed by brief reports on motorway hold-ups. The snag is that they tend to be out of date and don't always tell you in which direction the road is blocked. Also, you occasionally see roadside signs giving details of local stations to which you can tune for further updates of traffic news. These are well worth trying.

A further source of information may be at some service areas. Initially, four on the M1 are being equipped with TV Ceefax screens for giving continuous Teletext information about roadworks and traffic conditions. If the experiment proves worthwhile, others will follow.

Take even more care than usual in contra-flows.

Contra-flows

Contra-flows, when both streams of opposing traffic share one carriageway due to highway repairs, are a fact of motorway life. All are preceded by early warning signs that give drivers plenty of time to figure out from the symbols which lane or lanes will be closed and which will be free. Make your move into a free lane early, whilst traffic is still flowing fast.

As the traffic queues to squeeze into the reduced number of lanes it benefits nobody to play dog-in-the-manger. If you are in a 'free' lane then let any vehicle from the 'joining' lane slot in ahead of you. If everybody did that, even just for one vehicle each, most queues at bottlenecks would be greatly reduced.

The main advice to help cope safely with contra-flows is to take even more care than usual. When narrowed down to one or two lanes, traffic bunches up even more – so look well ahead, through the glass of the cars ahead, or if there is room, edge over just a few feet to get a better view along the stream. Maintain an increased stopping distance because when traffic slows in a contra-flow it tends to set off a chain-reaction of panic braking. Remember to keep on the straight and narrow – and that only a line of cones separates you from the opposing traffic. Both columns of vehicles may well be travelling at 70 mph or more, so the impact speed in a head-on crash could be a lethal 140 mph.

Looking ahead

Blessed is the driver who manages to look ahead and behind at the same time. He or she is aware, when forced to brake heavily by goings on ahead, of how close the following vehicles are and what lanes they are occupying. Consequently this driver is aware that, if a car or truck immediately behind is clearly not slowing quickly enough, a rear-end shunt may often be avoided by a smart lane switch to either right or left – in the latter case, maybe on to the hard shoulder without being illegal. This situation emphasizes once again the necessity of frequent use of the mirrors on the motorway; it enables one to have a good idea of the traffic *pattern* to the rear, so that only a quick confirmatory glance is needed should that particular emergency arise.

Another instance where use of the hazard flashers could be of real help to following traffic is if a vehicle ahead sheds some of its load or drops its exhaust system on the road, or one encounters some other sizeable object in the carriageway. The conspicuous signal warns even the most lethargic driver behind to be on the lookout for *something*.

Look out for debris on the road. Chunks of wrecked tyres from trucks are common, but not worth a dangerous swerve to avoid.

Finally, it is as well to have at least some idea in advance as to what you should do, or at least try to do, if you come on the scene of an accident, whether trivial or serious. If it is clearly the former, the best thing you can do is carry on driving. And remember, if you follow the scene around with your eyes as you pass, you may run smack into the back of the chap in front, doing the same thing but more slowly.

The same course of action should be followed where a more serious accident has happened some time previously and the emergency services are already in action at the

Badly secured loads can soon become road debris.

scene. You will only make things more difficult for them by hanging about.

If a serious accident has just happened, you may very well be able to help. As before, the first step must be to get on to the hard shoulder and switch on your hazard flashers. Then, circumstances will dictate whether you make for the nearest motorway telephone to summon an ambulance or lend a hand on the spot. Further advice is hard to give, owing to the enormous range of possibilities, but a point worth bearing in mind is that, unless you are a doctor or nurse, injured people should be left in their vehicles until expert help arrives, because well meaning attempts to move them may make their injuries worse. The only exception here is where fire breaks out and puts the victims' lives at risk. Do you carry a fire extinguisher in your car, van or truck? You may never need it but if you do you'll be thankful you spent those few pounds.

Meal on a motorway?

Hundreds of cans of custard, mushy peas and rice were once scattered over a 30-mile stretch of the M5 when a truck shed its load between Gloucester and Bristol.

3-wheeler

A Range Rover was driven for nearly four miles on three wheels after the front offside wheel came off when it collided with the central barrier on the M42 when being chased by three police cars. The chase started when police tried to stop the driver for a breath test near Redditch.

Auf Wiedersehn

A German tourist was flagged down on the M4 to be given a rather important message. He had left his wife behind at the Membury service area already 30 miles astern. What's the German for 'Thought I'd made it this time'?

8

BAD WEATHER

Extreme heat is something we rarely suffer from in Britain but almost every other weather extreme certainly can pose problems. Anyone who has driven on a motorway in heavy rain, for instance, will already be familiar with just how difficult conditions can become.

The first reason for this is that, to ensure directional stability of vehicles travelling at high speed and possibly changing lanes, most motorways are built with a straight crossfall.

Single-carriageway all-purpose roads usually have a pronounced camber, but on such roads most cars and commercial vehicles have a slight but definite tendency to veer off to the left. This effect would become even more pronounced on a heavily cambered motorway or even if the straight crossfall were increased.

So we have to live with the fact that surface water does not drain quickly. Moreover, the surfacing materials used – concrete in particular – are usually impervious to water, so even quite a light shower is not absorbed and most of it lies around until it evaporates.

To make matters worse, minor subsidences of the roadway are not uncommon, and they allow water to collect in puddles that can grow large enough to be called pools. Because of all the other surface water, the comparatively high speeds of approach and the generally reduced visibility in the wet, you can find yourself in or on one of these hazards almost before you are aware of it.

Aquaplaning

The use of 'on' in that last sentence is deliberate since at the higher speeds you may encounter the unnerving experience of *aquaplaning*. Water being incompressible, a tyre has either to deflect it or to pick it up in the tread grooves, squeegee style, carry it around and centrifuge it out (astern or into the wheel arches) if the rubber is to get a grip on the road. At high speeds, even with the best of tread patterns, there simply may not be enough time for that clearance to be made, so the tyre rides up on the film of water – yes, even though it may be carrying up to half a ton of car – and planes along like a speedboat.

Symptoms are easily recognized by the driver: the steering wheel jerks as the front wheels hit the water, then the control goes strangely light as a result of that effective film of lubricant between tyres and road. What happens next depends largely on you. If you react correctly, nothing serious will occur unless you happen to be cornering too fast for the conditions. If you panic, though, you may well be on the way to a major accident.

As when driving on ice (see later) the important thing is not to make any large or sudden movements on the steering wheel and neither to hit the brakes nor accelerate hard; any such action will almost certainly send you into a skid. If you just hold the wheel lightly, though, maintain a straight course and don't try to change your speed, all should be well. Within a few seconds at most you will be over the worst of the water and the tyres will be gripping again. It stands to reason, though, that if you have some steering lock on when they do, you may head swiftly off the carriageway.

The moral? Look ahead when there's a lot of standing water, reading the road even more closely than usual. And cut your speed to something at which aquaplaning could not occur in those conditions.

Spray – a major hazard

Our next problem posed by rain on motorways is the amount of it that flies about as clouds of spray. Even though we at last have legislation to reduce the spray from heavy commercial vehicles, the danger looks like being here to stay. All that water ejected by tyres has to go *somewhere*, and most of it goes out into the surrounding airspace – up to many gallons a minute of it from an 18-wheel artic on a bad day. The latest mudguards, with internal bristles and projections to catch water, are certainly an improvement but are far from being a cure, and older vehicles often have nothing at all at the rear.

Visibility is made even worse by the flat back of most big HGVs. This creates a powerful vortex which sucks in the water-laden air from all around and then emits it in huge eddying clouds.

Anyone who has tried to overtake a box-bodied artic travelling along at 60 mph in a rainstorm will know the situation only too well. It's like trying to get past a powerboat, peering into an apparently impenetrable wall of water and hoping there's nothing ahead. Of course, the truck *could* go slower and throw up less spray, but *we* could go slower too.

Is overtaking in those conditions really worth the risk? Remember that trite but true old saying 'Better to be a few minutes late in this world than a few years early in the next.' Passing at high speed in rain can be downright frightening, so why do it unless you really have to? Especially when on our crowded roads you will probably encounter the next truck in the queue and have to go through the whole traumatic experience again.

Aquaplaning and spray are major motorway hazards.

Spray thrown up by lorries is a major motorway menace.

Other watery dangers

Apart from aquaplaning and blind overtaking, rain poses the same problems on motorways as it does on ordinary roads. Grip is significantly reduced, and you can't tell in advance by how much, so you should allow substantially longer braking distances. Also, steering movements need to be made more smoothly than in the dry: a sudden twitch of the wheel at 60–70 mph can start a slide, especially if there's a strong cross-wind to help destabilise the car, and/or if the surface is slippery with oil or diesel fuel. The left-hand lane on long up-grades, though, often carries a labouring line of laden heavies.

When to use your lights

Remember to switch on your dipped headlamps as soon as heavy rain starts to fall, even in broad daylight. The law is far from precise as to just when they should go on, so you will have to use your own judgement, erring on the side of caution. Having the headlamps on makes you much more visible to preceding traffic which may well have rear windows and mirrors partially obscured by the rain, at a time when the driver's attention should really be concentrated on what's ahead, not what's behind.

Use your headlights, not just sidelights, as soon as

Dipped headlights must be used when visibility is below 100 metres.

visibility deteriorates substantially. One test of what constitutes 'substantially' – is whether the problem, be it rain, fog, mist, falling snow or whatever, prevents a clear view of the road ahead. That applies whether the horizon is a long way off or a large building just a short way ahead on an urban motorway. Remember that the purpose of headlights in this context is as much to enable you to be seen as to be able to see.

Keep the demisting going, also the rear-window heater, and even (unless your car's ventilation is very good) have the windows open a little to provide some fresh air circulation and so avoid the condensation that can otherwise insidiously start to obscure your view.

If your car has high-intensity rear lights, use them too – but only if visibility is really bad, as the law stipulates. They do have their disadvantages too: they can dazzle following drivers, especially when spray or rain is already accentuating glare, and they can be mistaken for brake lights or mask their warnings. In all but the worst seeing conditions, your normal tail lights are easily seen from astern.

As a guide such aids as high-intensity rear lights should only be used when few, if any, other vehicles are about. On crowded roads they are more likely to cause dazzle.

Drivers have been known to use those extra-bright rear lights to ward off someone following too closely – tailgating. This is understandable but short-sighted behaviour. Being aggressive is liable to provoke retaliation, so don't do it.

Don't place much reliance on the horn as a means of indicating your presence. Most cars will have all windows closed and probably the radio or tape player on. Use headlamp flashing instead – but only to indicate that you are there, not to pass a signal. Some drivers interpret a headlamp flash as meaning 'don't forget I'm here' while others take it to mean 'you can go – I'll make way for you'. Still others translate it as 'get out of my way!' With so much room for misunderstanding don't take chances.

At night, dip your headlights even for vehicles on a widely separated opposite carriageway. Except on right-hand curves the light can still dazzle them.

Fog

Fog (or mist, its more poetic-sounding junior partner) is a curse on motorways at any time, not least on account of its will-o'-the-wisp nature. You can go from clear, 100 per cent visibility into a patch of the wretched stuff with next to no warning, especially in dips and near water. Fortunately, some advances are being made with fog-sensing devices that will automatically switch on the motorway warning lights. This should at least reduce the likelihood of plunging headlong into an unexpected bank of fog.

The strongest 'Don't do it' warnings of all must be aimed at bad fog-time driving practices. 'Motorway pile up in fog' is almost a stock newspaper headline, and subsequent criticism from various official sources is just as predictable – albeit fully deserved. The greatest tragedy is that it is all so avoidable. No one *has* to drive too fast for the conditions. No one *has* to follow the vehicle in front blindly and closely. But so many drivers do, creating a high speed

In fog, keep a good distance behind the vehicles ahead.

nose-to-tail convoy that is heading for disaster as surely as any tribe of lemmings.

The remedy is simple: keep your speed down to a rate at which you can pull up within the distance that you can see to be clear ahead. And remember here that the obstruction in front, when you do spot it, may not be another vehicle trundling along a little slower than you; it may well be the back of an unlit *stationary* truck or car, already involved in an accident.

So don't be embarrassed at keeping your speed really low, even if this means crawling along at 5–10 mph in the inside lane. Quite possibly you will soon find some less patient driver keeping close station behind you, eager to overtake. Don't be 'pushed' by him – stay cool and sensible, and maintain that life-saving distance ahead between you and the next vehicle or the wall of fog.

The time to put on your high-intensity rear lights is when visibility in the fog is really bad and you are not aware of another vehicle behind you. *In extremis* you can even switch on your hazard flashers.

If you should be unfortunate enough to get involved in a motorway accident in fog and your car cannot be driven off the carriageway, the best advice is to 'Get out of there now!' Switch on the hazard flashers (if they are not already operating) and aim for the remote side of the hard shoulder as quickly as you can with safety; ears can be as useful as eyes in such circumstances.

As a final point on fog, ask yourself the old wartime question: 'Is my journey really necessary?' A motorway really is no place to be at such times and, if you can delay the trip or take another route, then for safety's sake why not do so?

Beware of crosswinds

One weather hazard you are unlikely to meet when there's fog about is a strong crosswind. Such winds affect some cars far more than others: some are virtually unaffected, remaining very stable, while others try to yaw off course and so have constantly to be steered, just as a yachtsman balances his boat with the helm against the wind force acting on the sails.

Remember that, when you come into the lee of a big truck on the motorway in a crosswind, you may at the time be subconsciously applying a few degrees of steering lock to hold the car straight. The car will then veer as it loses the side force and responds to that steering input. Then, when you finish overtaking, the car will veer the other way as it emerges into the wind again. This can be a daunting experience at first, so be ready for it.

Still more daunting is the sudden force that hits the car when you pass from a sheltered stretch of road into a full gale. At one place on the M23, where it comes out from a cutting, an easterly gale will move even quite a heavy car bodily sideways. Once again, the answer is not to go too fast for the conditions; below a certain critical speed the most ferocious of crosswinds is no longer a threat.

Motorways are often built up on embankments, and are therefore exposed to more wind than are ordinary roads. It's not just your vehicle which may be affected, of course. Make allowance for the fact that other drivers – particularly those in high-sided trucks and coaches – will be suffering too. This means giving them an extra wide berth when you overtake or just find yourself alongside.

Ice and snow

Unlike fog and crosswinds, these hazards are at least confined to the winter months, but that does not reduce the need to know how to cope with them. Perhaps surprisingly, ice is only a relatively infrequent problem on motorways, although it can be serious enough when it does occur. The high volume of traffic on many of these roads is enough in itself to break up frost and all but the most persistent black ice. The pressure of the tyres melts it, and the resulting water is then dispersed by succeeding tyres and the traffic-induced wind. And of course, gritting/salting lorries are usually quickly into action.

Where ice *does* occur – most commonly on the less heavily used slip-roads but also beneath bridges, where the sun comes late if at all, and on exposed stretches where wind-chill is likely – the same driving techniques apply as on any other road. That means gentle steering movements and extra braking distances to allow for light progressive retardation – in short, nothing that might provoke a slide.

Snow on the motorway is a different matter altogether. In other parts of the world, where the arrival of snow is not treated as an annual surprise, patrols stop all vehicles at the entry points when conditions are bad. If you do not have four-wheel drive or tyre chains, you simply are not allowed on the motorway. Why, the argument goes, should the unprepared block the road for everyone else?

In Britain, though, you may go ahead until the motorway is blocked by stalled or crashed vehicles. At that juncture, everyone just sits waiting to be rescued or for the obstructions to be removed.

To avoid becoming one of those obstructions or a motorway casualty of some other kind:

1 Ask yourself if you really need to venture out at all. If the answer is yes, carry on with points 2 to 10.

2 Have a spare pair of wheels shod with 'town and country' tyres, or chains or straps, ready for use at the driving end if things get really nasty.

3 Ensure you have plenty of fuel in case of a long hold-up, (when you will need to run the engine to keep the

heater working), and warm clothing in case the worst happens and you have to walk.

4 Carry a shovel, also grip mats of some kind with long strings so that you do not have to stop again to recover them.

5 Drive as if in fog or on ice – ie the motoring equivalent of walking on eggs.

6 Leave plenty of braking room not only for yourself but also for those behind you, if you can. The 38-tonne truck in your mirror will need a lot more slowing space than your car, so try to keep a cushion of distance between you.

7 Drive on dipped headlamps, day and night to make your vehicle as visible as possible. Use the high-intensity rear lights only if really needed – eg in heavy falling snow.

8 Allow for the disturbing visual effect of driving into such snow. Rest often, if only briefly, at service areas.

9 While keeping warm, ensure that fresh air is coming into the car, to help ward off drowsiness.

10 Keep in as high a gear and on as a small a throttle opening as possible. Too much 'right foot' and/or too low a gear will break traction, leading to wheelspin and, probably, the car slithering to an ignominious halt.

Why did they do it?
In October 1986 the M5 near Worcester had to be closed when hundreds of chickens tried to cross the road after escaping from a lorry that overturned.

Floral tribute
Saying it with flowers proved a McCartney smash in early 1987. Twenty thousand flowers, arranged to spell the name of Linda, wife of Paul McCartney, were set up in huge letters on a bank 150 yards from the M4, to advertise an exhibition of her photographs in Bath. However, the display so successfully attracted the attention of passing motorists that the flowers had to be removed after four vehicles collided.

9

MOTORCYCLING ON MOTORWAYS

Most experienced riders would agree that motorways are not the preferred environment for motorcycling. The advantages of the two wheeler are largely nullified, for its manoeuvrability must be used with restraint, the rider is vulnerable, and boredom can easily set in on a long run.

Given the choice of the M1 and, say, the A41 between London and the National Motorcycle Museum few would opt for the motorway, preferring the challenge of the traditional type of road. And as for the M25 London Orbital – definitely not the first choice for any rider during the rush hour.

Of course motorways can be used to advantage, when setting out on holiday, or to keep a business appointment, and this chapter reviews the preparation an advanced rider will make before setting out, and his use of Britain's motorway system.

The rider must be prepared for a greater degree of fatigue during a long motorway journey, especially if using an unfaired machine. You will require a lot of stamina to resist wind pressure, noise and buffeting from other vehicles' slipstreams, and you should therefore be fit, relaxed and prepared for the motorway's demands on your endurance and concentration. A heavy cold, a row with the boss, being late for an appointment – these are not burdens you want to carry on two wheels on a motorway.

Correct clothing

Your clothing must be correct for the climate and weather conditions you expect to encounter on route. Trainers, jeans and anorak are quite unsuitable for any serious rider on any road, let alone motorways. Leathers are preferred by many and, if they are your choice, you should ensure they are comfortably cut to suit the riding position, not for the local disco. A snug one-piece racing suit will be fine for 50 miles on your Mike Hailwood Replica, but may make your eyes water after 200 miles. And of course an oversuit, one or two piece, must be carried if not worn, because your leathers will not withstand heavy rain and spray. The traditional waxed cotton thornproof Barbour or Belstaff outfit is still the first choice for a great number of riders and if you don't mind putting up with the tendency to make the rest of your clothes grubby it is still one of the best alternatives to leathers and oversuit. A third type of weatherproof has become increasingly popular, using PVC coated or nylon materials, typified by Rukka and Motomod. You need to take extra care in handling these because they are more easily snagged and torn. Also, being impervious to moisture, they keep perspiration in as effectively as they keep rain out.

Your helmet and visor are of paramount importance and a good fit is essential at motorway speeds. You must keep the visor free of misting and one of the proprietary anti-fog compounds will help. The visor (or goggles) should provide a good seal or after a few miles in heavy rain you will have as much spray inside as raindrops outside. And remember, you can't stop to clean visor or goggles very easily – a Vee-wipe or a patch of chamois on a glove finger will help to keep your view clear. Don't forget to treat your spectacles, if worn, with anti-fog at the same time as you attend to the visor. Night time compounds all these problems and in darkness you will have to reduce speed.

When the weather is cold you must keep warm. Electrically heated gloves or grips can prevent an experienced rider from turning into a numbed automaton. Handlebar mittens are a cheaper practical alternative, even if unfashionable.

Preparing for your journey

The machine needs to be thoroughly checked over before any motorway journey, and you should not take for granted the reliability of the modern multi or single, any more than you would if you happen to be a British bike enthusiast for whom the old style check is second nature. Pay close attention to the condition of your tyres, the amount of tread depth and the pressures.

Choice of a motorway for a journey may be for the start of a holiday tour, which will mean a full pannier and topbox load, with perhaps a tent strapped on, and possibly a passenger. You must increase tyre pressures substantially over those specified for solo riding or the tyres will overheat and wear rapidly. Your machine's handbook and the tyre makers' literature should be consulted.

The size of machine will determine the load that can be handled and you should bear in mind that a fully laden 250 cc tourer will be hard put to maintain station with HGVs, let alone keep pace with the company Sierras in the outer lanes.

If you run a multi-cylinder cruiser or superbike, be it Gold Wing, Kawasaki GTR, or BMW K100LT, you will still have enough power to out accelerate most other vehicles, even when carrying the maximum permitted load, but remember that the handling could be radically changed by the extra weight it is carrying.

Adjust or modify your mirrors to give a clear rearward view.

You must also turn your attention to chains, water/oil levels, lights and indicators, control cables and levers, and make sure they are all correctly adjusted.

It is an unwelcome trend of fashion that nearly all modern faired machines are fitted with badly positioned mirrors which give a superb view of your shoulders, elbows or your passenger. As an advanced rider you must adjust, or if necessary modify, the mountings of your mirrors to give a clear view of the road behind you. The little 'overtaker' convex mirrors are some help but are no substitute for good mirrors.

The small size of the solo motorcycle in comparison with that of other motorway users makes conspicuity aids essential.

The yellow reflective Sam Browne type belt is as good as any, although some riders prefer a waistcoat or a tabard of reflective or fluorescent material.

However, do not assume even if your machine resembles a Christmas tree with lights, reflective strips and a bright paint job, that other drivers will automatically see you.

Whatever your views on the use of headlights, you should switch on your dipped beam when joining the motorway. Hence its setting needs checking to ensure it does not dazzle other road users, and you need to carry a spare bulb in your toolkit. Your kit will include puncture repair outfit, spare plugs, clutch and throttle cables and a torch that works.

Joining and leaving the motorway

Joining and leaving the motorway you can use the acceleration potential of the modern high performance machine to advantage, but it must not be a substitute for correct roadcraft. The most vital part of advanced technique is your ability to read the road and the traffic patterns both ahead and behind. Your mirror work must be impeccable and should not be hindered by badly positioned mirrors, as mentioned above.

If you ever have the good fortune to travel with a Police Class One rider you cannot fail to be impressed by his total awareness of what is happening all around him,

Advanced driving is about total awareness.

based on highly trained forward observation skills and mirror use. The 'Lifesaver' on motorways is a contentious subject, but you should not rely on it to compensate for poor mirror work, even though there will be times when you need to give a shoulder check before changing lanes. It makes sense to consider these checks much earlier than on other roads, and you should not attempt lifesavers when following a family saloon with dangling dollies on show while its driver is trying to summon up enough courage to merge with the inner lane.

Advanced riding is all about total awareness, and you can find opportunities to plan your course even before venturing on the sliproad. Your eye level is superior to that of most car drivers and you can use it to observe traffic patterns and flow; for example, if the motorway is approached via a bridge or embankment. If you assess the traffic in advance correctly, you will be able to blend smoothly with it from the slip-road and acceleration lane.

On preparing to leave a motorway, as per Highway Code paragraph 185, of course, you will find that your good view, the flexibility of acceleration/braking and small size of your machine will assist you in choosing your exit path in good time when a suitable gap in the inner lane traffic opens up. Here again, good mirror work will allow you to blend easily before the slip-road itself is reached. You must be alert to a danger that can arise on sliproads of motorways near car ferries. There have been several occasions when cars or lorries bearing foreign registrations have been encountered coming the wrong way on a slip-road, especially when the slip-road is approached by a two-lane carriageway marked out for two-way traffic.

When entering Service Areas you should take special care near other vehicles in the car parks. There will be drivers who are fatigued or harassed by children. Park your machine near the buildings, preferably in a slot in a corner, where it will be less easily knocked over.

On the motorway

Riding along the motorway you will maintain your forward and rear observation at a high level. On a sunny day with not much traffic you might be tempted to review your roadcraft, your bank balance or your choice at the next service area, but even in good riding conditions you must *concentrate*. The motorway lacks many of the features that keep your mind alert, the view is monotonous, scenery is often shut out by embankments or fences, and it is all too easy for the mind to wander. On four wheels, however inexcusable, you might get away with a second's day-dreaming. On a motorcycle you might wake up in hospital.

You must know the precise meaning of the motorway signs, and what the different coloured reflective studs indicate. You will find the practice of the Riding Plan – what you can see, what you cannot see and what you might expect to happen – a worthwhile aid to concentration. You can back this up with the IAM system of control and turn a tiresome journey into a mobile chess game, selecting your course to anticipate the traffic ahead and the rear, watching for merging vehicles at junctions and so on.

Extreme weather conditions

As an experienced rider you will be ready for extremes of weather conditions. Taking the worst of the weather from a rider's viewpoint, namely snow, ice, and fog; if you take the trouble to find out about conditions on your chosen route you can often make progress. Most motorways are given more attention in winter to keep them open, traffic tends to be lighter and it *can* be practical to cover long distances on two wheels. A word with an HGV driver who has just arrived can often update your knowledge better than the local TV or radio forecasts. There will be times when no sensible rider will venture on to motorways and you will then consider using car or public transport, or stay at home to catch up on some overdue service job on the bike.

Fog is an extreme hazard for the rider because although you generally have a better view than drivers, the behaviour of other motorway users will put you continually at risk. If the traffic streams are dense and slow-moving in continuous fog, you are comparatively safe, but patchy fog interspersed with sunshine – a typical London Orbital feature – can present you with intolerable danger, and you should leave the motorway. Rain from light drizzle to tropical intensity will require you to assess constantly the surface for adhesion and grip and to keep your visor/goggles clear. Spray is an ever-worsening problem and may prevent you maintaining your position in a traffic stream; you must drop back until a clear view can be obtained. You will be alert to aquaplaning and water-logged brakes and you should apply both brakes frequently to clear the water film that forms on the discs.

All machines are adversely affected by strong winds, and cross winds on a motorway can cause you a lot of difficulty. Some faired machines are more stable and give better tyre adhesion, but other fairings can adversely affect handling and you should know the characteristics of your particular model. Strong winds cause turbulent 'bow waves' and slipstreams around high-sided vehicles and you should make allowances for buffeting by leaving up to a lane's clear width when overtaking in these conditions.

Other hazards

You must be alert for physical road conditions because, apart from surface water, spilled diesel or oil and potholes, there tends to be a lot of debris on our motorways – anything from thrown tyre treads to beer cans and bottles. To a car driver these are an inconvenience, but to you they can be a recipe for disaster unless seen in good time.

One can seldom complete a motorway journey without encountering roadworks, but they offer less frustration to the two-wheeler's journey. You should consider sensible filtering when safe to do so, taking care not to upset other road users. Use of the hard shoulder unless permitted by roadwork signs is illegal and not at all sensible. If you display courtesy and proceed unobtrusively, the car or lorry driver ahead will often ease over to allow you to make progress. Watch out for changes in surfaces at roadworks, and of road levels, for builders' debris and displaced traffic cones. The so-called 'planed surface' is particularly destabilising, with its corrugations, and must be ridden over with care.

As an advanced rider you will have to contend with high traffic density and the resulting aggression that it all too often generates. In conclusion these situations are worth a little thought.

High-speed, high-density traffic on motorways can be a nightmare for even the most experienced rider, and when aggravated by heavy rain and poor visibility becomes an unacceptable risk. You would be well advised to leave the motorway at the next exit and use an alternative non-motorway route. This is common sense, not defeatism, because any attempt you make to maintain station in a stream of nose-to-tail vehicles at 60–70 mph is fraught with danger. The average driver just will not give you enough room to permit safe braking on a wet carriageway. These problems are compounded at junctions because the traffic pattern becomes unstable as drivers dive too late for slip-roads. Hence it is better to avoid these conditions and use your machine's flexibility and small size to continue on the nearby A and B routes. You should have a map covering the area in your panniers or top box, naturally.

Sometimes a traffic pattern develops to help you. As most drivers regard the outer lane as the fast lane, a triangular wedge of traffic progresses along the motorway at around or above the legal limit. This leaves the middle and inner lanes less densely populated, and gives you room to make progress without illegally passing on the inside.

Keeping up standards

Finally, it is a sad fact that driving standards on all our roads are drifting downwards, with aggression becoming more and more evident. You must allow for this and redouble your efforts to ride defensively. Even safe, permissible, filtering using your roadcraft will engender an aggressive response from some road users and you must not inflame the situation. The last role you want to assume is that of toreador; it's a spectacular profession but its practitioners get hurt.

So, even if it is tempting for you to baulk someone you should give way, knowing that before long you can more than match his progress when the traffic opens up. Far better to aspire to being a shepherd, regarding the flock of sheep ahead as something to be handled with care so that you can find the gaps you need to progress out of danger.

If you exhibit a predictable riding pattern, positioning your machine where it does not worry or threaten other drivers, very often you will establish a brief rapport. That driver ahead will ease over a little, settle down and let you pass. Similarly, at the inevitable hold-up, you might be able to exchange a nod or word or two with the driver alongside, so that when the traffic moves he'll give you a gap to use. A wave or salute will leave him in a better frame of mind to deal with the problems of driving on four wheels, while you *enjoy* two-wheeler freedom ahead.

Punter

An Irish punter decided a walk would help him sober up after a good day at Cheltenham races, and the wide road with the pleasant grass verge looked ideal. The celebrant was picked up by the police after staggering two miles – along the hard shoulder of the M5. He was taken to his hotel and put to bed.

10

EXPERT COMMENT

IAM examiners are highly experienced and perceptive drivers who cover considerable mileages every year, quite a lot of it on motorways, in all possible conditions of traffic and weather. They are all past or present Class One police drivers, hence they are in a better position than most road users to comment and advise on motorway driving. The Institute's Chief Examiner, Ted Clements, therefore asked his staff for brief items on their view of motorway behaviour.

What follows is a selection of the best subdivided into six main categories. The two attracting the biggest number of replies were speed/distance assessment and lane discipline, as might be expected.

General

Motorways' original conception as fast inter-city routes no longer applies. The majority use today is by the short-distance businessman commuter, in an unprepared car, under pressure and lacking concentration.

Although each carriageway is only a large one-way street, all the judgement and skill required on normal roads has to be practised, including noticing traffic conditions in the other carriageway.

Motorway driving is an act frequently performed in the wrong lane, at too great a speed and far too close to the vehicle ahead.

Because of the relative ease of driving on motorways, most drivers relax too much – hence poor lane discipline, inability to recognise danger quickly enough, shunt incidents, lack of attention to speed and so on.

Despite education and legislation, there will always be that acknowledged 15 per cent of the driving public who are irresponsible idiots when in charge of a vehicle.

Speed/distance assessment

The majority drive too close and fail to comply with correct lane procedures.

During peak periods on congested motorways, drivers are aggressive, show poor lane discipline and follow too close at high speeds.

Most drivers travel too close to one another, not allowing sufficient safety margins for the higher speeds or for weather or road conditions. They overtake with insufficient restraint and do not comply with matrix signals, the majority apparently not knowing what they mean.

Too fast, too close, no room for error.

The small speed differentials between the various classes of vehicles are the cause of bunching which prevents drivers from 'keeping their distance'.

Traffic travels too close, allowing insufficient reaction time.

The 70 mph speed limit should be abolished because it encourages bunching: vehicle intervals are too close under all conditions.

Many drivers travel far too fast for their capabilities, ignoring the rules and signs of the Highway Code.

Too many motorway users drive too close and too fast, regardless of weather and road conditions.

Most motorists could exercise better judgement of speed and distance when joining a motorway, instead of just pressing on regardless.

The level of attention never appears to keep up with the speed of the vehicles.

Many drive too fast for their ability, and too close to the vehicle ahead.

When one is travelling at 103 feet per second (70 mph) things happen quickly.

Lane discipline

Most motorway drivers seem to think you have to buy a special ticket to use Lane 1.

The most irritating problem is lane misuse, so my message to all drivers is 'learn to use the correct lane'.

My chief motorway dislikes are failure to use Lane 1, causing bunching, driving too close together in the other lanes.

My pet hate is the driver who joins the motorway, gets into the middle lane and goes back to sleep.

British motorway driving is very poor, due to lack of training in lane discipline and excessive speed of HGVs and coaches.

There is bad lane discipline, poor following positioning and no consideration for others . . . a lack of mirror checks, yet an overtaking driver expects the other driver to know he is there. Most motorway drivers' motto is the 11th Commandment – 'if in doubt, flat out'.

Educate the middle-lane road hog – get him over to the left.

Deplorable lane discipline and the failure to keep a safe distance from the vehicle in front.

Lack of correct lane discipline.

Educate for lane discipline and against lane hogging – overtake and pull back, not hold back.

One of the worst features of motorway driving is hogging the middle lane; drive on the left, except when overtaking.

'Lane discipline' doesn't seem to feature in most drivers' vocabulary.

Aggression

Motorway driving lacks professionalism and is too aggressive and selfish.

It's not the motorways that kill – it's the killers that drive on the motorways.

Heavy goods lorries signal, then pull out to overtake whether the way is clear or not.

Observation, concentration and anticipation

The majority of drivers travel too close to the vehicle ahead and also exercise very little observation, concentration and anticipation.

There is a general lack of concentration, observation and anticipation.

Some very good drivers and many average drivers, all trying to anticipate and avoid the dangerous antics of too many selfish idiots.

It is equally important to know what is happening behind as in front.

Remember the rear-view mirror and use it every 10 to 15 seconds.

Your safety may depend more on the driver behind than in front of you; watch your mirror closely and give him early clear signals.

One of the troubles is a general lack of early forward observation and planning in relation to potential hazards ahead.

Few people are qualified to drive at high speed due to lack of 'extended observation'.

A mixed bag

When visibility is poor – eg in the half-light of dawn or dusk, or in spray – I am appalled by the number of motorists who overtake with either just sidelights or no lights at all.

Motorways are very safe, but never become so complacent that you forget to expect the unexpected.

*There is at present no education for motorway driving – just experience. Isn't it time we **trained** people to use motorways correctly?*

11

MOTORWAY DRIVING COMMENTARY

We asked Ted Clements, Chief Examiner of the IAM, to give a commentary drive on the motorway. In effect, it's thinking aloud and gives a useful insight into how advanced techniques work in practice.

'I'm joining Britain's busiest motorway, the M25, approaching it via a slip-road from the M4. On the road ahead of me are those white hatchings used on busy junctions to keep you in your chosen lane, so I shall stay in mine.

'Before reaching them, though, still on the slip road, I take a good look in my mirror. Only a heavy goods vehicle some distance astern on the motorway, so it's safe to join the left-hand lane after the usual quick glance over the shoulder in case a car was in my blind-spot earlier.

'This is a very busy stretch with the maximum speed limit of 70 mph, and the surface is good dry tarmac. I'm catching up a couple of heavies in my lane and am being overtaken by quite a lot of traffic on my offside, but initially I keep my speed down to 50–55 while getting used to the conditions. Since I'm closing on the heavies, a glance in the mirror: following traffic is a fair way back but could benefit from a signal, so indicate right and look again in mirror – OK to move out and pass this first slow-moving truck.

'A lot of stuff is now overtaking me in the outside lane, many of the cars clearly exceeding the speed limit but that's their business. Another mirror glance: lots of traffic behind me and plenty of slower movers in the nearside lane unable to get out into the middle one. Hold speed at about 70, not getting too close to that chap in front, and now there's a gap in the inner lane; the mirror tells me it's safe to pull over but I mustn't carve up the truck I've just passed.

'Hello! Brake lights ahead, but why? Nothing to worry about – just the volume of traffic, it seems. There's the sign for an appropriate junction, so watch out for vehicles on the off-side leaving things late for getting to the slip-road. I'm keeping in the nearside lane and being very vigilant all the time.

'Safely past the exit slip, now I must be careful about the entry one coming up ahead, especially that large red car which seems determined to barge straight out and across to the outside lane at whatever cost. A string of inner-lane heavies ahead, so it's mirror again: nothing for some distance behind, so signal, wait a few seconds and take a second look astern. Safe to pull out into the middle lane, accelerating gently to 65–70 while keeping an intermittent watch on cars to my offside and those heavies on the other side.

'A car in front signalled *left* and is now moving out to its *right*. A bit ahead, too, a chap in a Metro is signalling his intention to pull out into my lane, so ease up a shade until I'm sure he has seen me and not through me – fine, he's holding back to let me go through.

'There's a Road Works sign ahead (for 3 miles), so ease off again and take stock of what the others are up to. Still not sure which lane is closed, if any, but now we've a second sign saying "Road narrows from right". Seeing a lot of brake lights coming on up the road, and a bit of bobbing and weaving, I'm reducing my speed to about 40 and keeping a good mirror look-out behind.

'Now another sign, "Temporary lane closure" on the offside, so the drill is keep in lane, use the mirror frequently and continue to slow down to about 20. The traffic has settled again, except for one Clever Charlie who's driving on the hard shoulder, so watch out for him when he decides to rejoin the carriageway. "Road clear" sign ahead at last but better to hang back and wait for the mass exodus. It's just like the starting grid at Brands Hatch

– everyone for himself. Now we're clear of the roadworks and I can safely build up speed once more.

'There's a car ahead parked on the hard shoulder with its flasher on; the driver's changing a *nearside* wheel so no real problem. Brake lights coming on again ahead – what's it this time? Oh yes, a police car perched on its little eminence. Amazing what a sobering effect this has on most of the drivers, and they'll keep to their safe speed for a while too.

Hazard ahead

'Still travelling in the middle lane, at the maximum limit, because on the inside one there's a small builder's pick-up with a large load and a flapping tarpaulin – just the thing to give a wide berth! Now a change of road surface, to concrete which is good for braking but bad for tyre noise. Mirror again: lots of traffic behind and one car getting

Joining Britain's busiest motorway, the M25.

rather close but I'm not easily intimidated. The next mirror glance shows he's backed off a bit but I mustn't forget about him.

'Up comes the Guildford A3 sign – very welcome to me since it spells home – or very nearly. Even so, must still concentrate and keep my wits about me. Half a mile on, here's the second sign to a look in the mirror; all clear – indicate left and pause briefly before moving over into the inside lane and beginning to reduce speed. Passing the 300 marker I'm again signalling left ready to swing away into the slip-road.

Normal roads

'Up the slope and continuing to slow, using the mirror and signalling right towards Guildford, keeping to the right of the slip-road of course. This roundabout's one to approach with great caution from the M25 eastbound carriageway owing to poor sight lines. Now I'm off the motorway and on to the ordinary road system, so must make a conscious effort to adapt to the changed environment and speed limits'

Record jam

In 1985, during a holiday weekend, roadworks and accidents on the M1 produced a 40-mile traffic jam from junction 13 at Milton Keynes to junction 18 at Rugby.

Freak accident

A driver was killed by his own car in a freak accident on the M62 near Dewsbury, Yorkshire, in November 1986. He'd got out of his Vauxhall in a hold-up when another vehicle shunted his car into him.

PART TWO
ADVANCED DRIVING TESTS

12

THE ADVANCED DRIVING TEST

The Institute . . .

. . . was founded by motorists from all walks of life with the common aim of making our roads safer by raising driving standards. It is controlled by a Council elected because of their expertise in various spheres of motoring. They represent accident prevention authorities, medicine, motor racing, the motor industry and trade, driving schools, magistrates, the motoring Press, other organisations, the Institute's own area Groups and Members of Parliament. The IAM's activities have been endorsed by successive Transport Ministers since it started. As an expert organisation its opinions on driving safety matters are regularly sought by the Government. Indeed, one of our main aims is to represent the views of skilled, responsible motorists to the authorities. To this end, each new member of the Institute becomes a valuable addition to the campaign for better driving and safer roads.

The advanced test has been adopted by the Army at home and abroad and by more than 300 companies as a stringent check on driving skill.

So far over 280,000 motorists have taken the test and 65 per cent of them have passed and joined the Institute. Of these successful drivers one in four is a woman, with a success rate in the test similar to the men.

How good a driver are *you*?

Very expert, perhaps, but are you sure? You may have passed the Government's driving test first time and with ease. This, however, is a very basic, elementary examination. Passing it should be merely the beginning of your motoring career; the starting point in the acquisition of mature driving skills.

Happily, most motorists realise this and there comes a time when they want to reassure themselves that their skill is developing along the right lines. This is what the Institute of Advanced Motorists is all about. Founded in 1956, it is a non-profit-earning organisation registered as a charity and founded to promote road safety by encouraging motorists to take a pride in their driving. By taking the Institute test they can measure the progress they have made since throwing away their L-plates.

The test, which lasts for 90 minutes, is something which any motorist of reasonable experience and skill should be able to pass without difficulty. But whether the candidates pass or fail they learn a great deal from the ex-Police drivers who hold Advanced Police certificates and conduct the tests on some 137 different routes located all over Britain.

Skill with responsibility . . . that is what the IAM is out to promote. If every driver had the ability to pass the IAM test and the self-discipline to employ its standards at all times, there would be a dramatic drop in the number of road casualties – averaging 350,000 a year at present.

The test currently costs £18.50 and if you pass you will become a member of the Institute for an annual subscription of £7.50 including VAT.

Each test route measures about 35–40 miles and incorporates road conditions of all kinds including congested urban areas, main roads, narrow country lanes and residential streets.

You are not expected to give a display of fancy driving. On the contrary, our examiners hope you will handle your car in the steady workmanlike way in which you should drive day in, day out. They don't, for example, expect exaggeratedly slow speeds or excessive signalling.

They want to see candidates observe all speed limits and drive with due regard to road, traffic and weather conditions but they also want to see them drive briskly and not be afraid to cruise at the legal limit when circumstances permit.

You will be asked to reverse around a corner and to make a hill start. There will be one or two spot checks on your powers of observation. There are no trick questions, no attempts to catch you out and you are not even required to give a running commentary at any time (although you are free to do so if you wish to make extra clear your ability to 'read the road').

Here in greater detail are some of the things our examiners look for and comment on in their test reports:

Acceleration
Smooth and progressive? Excessive or insufficient? Is acceleration used at the right time and place?

Braking
Smooth and progressive or late and fierce? Are the brakes used in conjunction with mirror and/or signals? Are road, traffic and weather conditions taken into account?

Clutch control
Are engine and road speeds properly co-ordinated when changing gear? Does the candidate slip or ride the clutch? Does he coast with the clutch disengaged?

Gear changing
Is it a smooth change action, without jerking? If automatic transmission is fitted does the driver make full use of it?

Use of gears
Are the gears correctly selected and used? Is the right gear selected before reaching a hazard?

Steering
Is the wheel held correctly with the hands at quarter to three or ten to two positions? Does the driver pass the wheel through his hands? Use of the 'cross arms' technique except when manoeuvring in confined spaces is not recommended.

Driving position
Is the candidate alert or does he slump at the wheel? Does he nonchalantly rest an arm on the door while driving?

Observation
Does he 'read' the road ahead and show a good sense of anticipation? Does he show the ability to judge speed and distance?

Concentration
Does the driver keep his attention on the road? Does he allow himself to be distracted easily?

Maintaining progress
Bearing in mind the road, traffic and weather conditions, does the driver keep up a reasonable pace and maintain good progress?

Obstruction
Is the candidate careful not to obstruct other vehicles, by driving too slowly, taking up the wrong position on the road or failing to anticipate and react correctly to the traffic situation ahead?

Positioning
Does the driver keep to the correct part of the road, especially when approaching hazards?

Lane discipline
Does he keep to the appropriate lane? Is he careful not to straddle white lines?

Observation of road surfaces
Does the driver keep an eye on the road surface, especially in bad weather, and does he watch out for slippery conditions?

Traffic signals
Are signals, signs and road markings observed, obeyed and approached correctly? Does the driver show courtesy at pedestrian crossings?

Speed limits and other legal requirements
Are they observed? The examiner cannot condone breaches of the law.

Overtaking
Is this carried out safely and decisively, maintaining the right distance from other vehicles and using the mirror, signals and gears correctly?

Hazard procedure and cornering
Are road and traffic hazards coped with properly? Are bends and corners taken in the right manner?

Mirror
Does the candidate frequently use the mirror? Does he use

it especially in conjunction with his signals and before changing speed or course?

Signals
Are turn indicator signals and hand ones when needed given at the right place and in good time? Are the horn and headlight flasher used in accordance with the Highway Code?

Restraint
Does the candidate show reasonable restraint – but not indecision – at the wheel?

Consideration
Is sufficient consideration and courtesy shown to other road users?

Car sympathy
Does he treat the car with care? Does he overstress it? Perhaps by revving the engine needlessly or by fierce braking?

Manoeuvring
Finally are manoeuvres such as reversing performed smoothly and competently?

These, then are the main requirements of the advanced test. They probably call for no more than the skill you use in your everyday motoring. But if you would like to know more on any of the points you should look again at the Highway Code and read more in *Advanced Motoring*, the IAM's own driving manual; *Roadcraft*, the Police drivers' text book; and for motorcyclists *Advanced Motorcycling*, which is the Institute's own manual and *Motor Cycle Roadcraft*, the Police drivers' manual. All are available from bookshops or direct from the Institute of Advanced Motorists.

At the end of your test your examiner will give you an expert view of your skill and responsibility at the wheel. There may be praise and certainly constructive criticism will be offered; the Institute aims at being entirely honest with you. Occasionally, for instance, a driver is found to have developed a potentially dangerous fault of which he is completely unaware. A quiet word from the examiner may help him correct it. You will not be failed for minor faults.

Who can take the test?

Anyone with a full British or EEC driving licence providing that he has not been convicted of a serious traffic offence in the last three years. You can take the test in almost any car which you provide yourself, in most vans, trucks and motorcycles. US and Allied servicemen can also apply.

Disabled drivers

Disabled drivers are welcome as candidates providing they use a suitably adapted car.

Where can I take the test?

Probably close to your home. A list of Institute test routes is shown for you to choose from. The examiner will meet you at a pre-arranged rendezvous. Tests are available from Monday to Friday.

Can I prepare?

Yes, of course. There are many books available on advanced driving, among them the manuals that we mentioned earlier. Also, many professional driving instructors are Institute members and can coach pupils up to the standard of the advanced test. In addition, you can ask your local council's road safety officer for details of advanced driving courses in your areas, or contact your local Members' Group. (List available on request.)

Who are the examiners?

They are all holders of the Police advanced driving certificate. This means that they have passed the stiffest test of driving ability in Britain.

When you pass . . .

. . . the test and become a member of the IAM these are among the benefits you can have:

Badge
The right to display the Institute's badge on your car, providing visible proof of the standard you have set yourself.

Insurance
An introduction to motor insurers who may, subject to a satisfactory proposal, give special terms.

Magazine
A motoring magazine, *Milestones*, produced especially for IAM members and written by and for people who take a keen interest in driving and cars, is published every four months.

Local Groups
The chance to meet other men and women who share your outlook on motoring, if you decide to join one of the Institute's local Groups and take part in the road safety driving and social events which they organise.

Caravan and towing test
A test for drivers towing trailers and caravans is available to members. Please ask for details.

Application forms
On the next pages are application forms for the advanced test – one for your own use and a second for a friend or relative.

Commercial vehicles and motor tricycles
If you want to take the test in a commercial vehicle or motor tricycle, just phone or write to the Institute for the special form required. Details of solo motorcycle tests are given further on.

Test routes

Aberdeen	Folkestone	Porthmadog
Aylesbury	Galashiels	Portsmouth
Ayr	Glasgow	Preston
Banff	Grantham	Reading
Bangor	Greenock	Retford
Barnsley	Grimsby	Ripon
Bedford	Guildford	Rotherham
Belfast	Harrogate	Scarborough
Berwick-on-	Hartlepool	Scunthorpe
Tweed	Haverfordwest	Sheffield
Birkenhead	Hereford	Shrewsbury
Birmingham	Huddersfield	Southampton
Blackpool	Hull	Southend
Bodmin	Huntly	St Austell
Bolton	Inverness	St Helens
Boston	Ipswich	Staines
Bournemouth	Isle of Man	Stockport
Bradford	Isle of Wight	Stoke-on-Trent
Bridgend	Kendal	Stowmarket
Brighton	Kettering	Sunderland
Bristol	Ladybank	Swansea
Bude	Leeds	Swindon
Burton-on-Trent	Leicester	Taunton
Bury St Edmunds	Lichfield	Truro
Cambridge	Lincoln	Tunbridge Wells
Canterbury	Liverpool	Wakefield
Cardiff	Londonderry	Walsall
Carlisle	Luton	Watford
Chelmsford	Maidstone	Wetherby
Cheltenham	Manchester	Wick
Chester	Mansfield	Widnes
Chichester	Middlesbrough	Wigan
Chorley	Newark	Winchester
Colwyn Bay	Newcastle	Windsor
Coventry	Newmarket	Woking
Crawley	Newport	Wolverhampton
Crewe	Northampton	Worcester
Darlington	Norwich	Worksop
Debenham	Nottingham	Worthing
Derby	Oban	Yeovil
Dorchester	Okehampton	York

Dumfries
Dundee
Dunoon
Edinburgh
Elgin
Exeter

Oxford
Penrith
Perth
Peterborough
Plymouth

London:
Barnes
Crystal Palace
Harrow
Wanstead

West Germany *(HM Forces and British Nationals only)*

Bielefeld
Gutersloh

Hanover
Paderborn

Rheindahlen
Sennelager

Cyprus *(HM Forces and British Nationals only)*
Akrotiri   Larnaca

---

20 years on

When the M1 was 20 years old, the AA claimed that its patrols were still dealing with terrified drivers who got on to the motorway by mistake and thought they had to drive to Birmingham before they could turn round. Some drivers still managed to drive up exit roads and rushed down the motorway in the wrong direction, behaviour matched by a group of nuns found on the hard shoulder near Toddington sitting around their picnic table.

13

THE ADVANCED MOTORCYCLE DRIVING TEST

The first brochure issued by the Institute of Advanced Motorists in 1956 said:

'Whilst the initial scheme (for motor cars) does not cover motorcyclists, the Institute intends to include them at a later date.' It was not until November 1975 that a decision was taken by the IAM Council to extend the advanced driving test to solo motorcyclists, who, on reaching the necessary standards, can become members of the Institute on exactly the same footing as those who have qualified by way of cars or commercial vehicles.

With the upsurge in the popularity of motorcycling has come, over the last few years, a tragic increase in death and injuries to motorcyclists. It has been proved that advanced driving methods properly applied can reduce accidents, and with this in mind the commencement of an advanced driving test could be of great benefit to all road users. The advanced motorcycle driving test (yes – officially you do 'drive' a motorcycle) was devised by the Institute and the standard set was arrived at by motorcyclists. Those invited by the Institute to form a Standards Committee included RAC/ACU, Instructors, the motorcycling press, motorcycling bodies and Class One Police Certificate holders.

The Test

The test is based on well known 'Roadcraft' principles, and is of the 'pursuit' type with the examiner following you on another motorcycle and observing your actions, positioning, sign observation, and signals – all the features which will ensure that you are on the right part of the road at the correct speed and in the correct gear. All the examiners hold an advanced police certificate. The road test takes about 50 minutes and a further 20 minutes will be required for off-the-road tests designed to test slow riding ability. The balance of the 90-minute period is spent in briefing and debriefing, during which time the examiner will have a thorough discussion with the candidate about any faults revealed during the test.

The candidate will be given verbal instruction to the route to be followed and stops will be made from time to time to allow further route directions. It is stressed that any errors in following a route have no bearing whatever on the outcome of the test.

Who can take the test?

Anyone with a full substantive British or EEC driving licence, providing that he or she has not been convicted recently for a serious traffic offence. You must use a road-worthy motorcycle in the 200 cc class or above. Tests cannot be carried out using mopeds. Helmet and goggles, or helmet with visor incorporated, and gloves must be worn whilst riding.

Where can I take the motorcycle test?

Probably quite close to your home. The Institute has 79 test routes as follows:

Aberdeen	Edinburgh	Nottingham
Aylesbury	Exeter	Oxford
Bangor	Glasgow	Peterborough
Bedford	Gloucester	Plymouth
Belfast	Guildford	Porthmadog
Birkenhead	Harlow	Portsmouth
Birmingham	Harrow	Preston
Blackpool	Haverfordwest	Sheffield
Bodmin	Hertford	Shrewsbury
Boston	Hull	Southampton
Bournemouth	Inverness	Southend

Bradford	Ipswich	Stafford
Bridgend	Isle of Man	Stevenage
Brighton	Isle of Wight	Stockport
Bristol	Kendal	Stoke-on-Trent
Cambridge	Kettering	Sunderland
Canterbury	Lincoln	Swansea
Carlisle	Liverpool	Swindon
Chelmsford	Maidstone	Taunton
Cheltenham	Manchester	Truro
Chester	Mansfield	Wakefield
Chichester	Newcastle-on-	Wanstead
Colwyn Bay	Tyne	Worcester
Coventry	Newport (Gwent)	Worksop
Crystal Palace	Northallerton	Worthing
Derby	Northampton	York
Dorchester	Norwich	

Other routes will be opening in the near future. Tests are conducted on weekdays, or by special arrangements, Saturdays (Sunday does not provide a consistent traffic pattern) and the local examiner will contact you to arrange a mutually convenient date and time.

How do I prepare for the test?

You can read 'Motorcycle Roadcraft' (obtainable from the Institute or HMSO). The Institute has published its own manual, 'Advanced Motorcycling'. For more practical instruction you should contact your local Road Safety Officer, as he may be able to put you in touch with the evening class organisers in 'Better Riding' subjects, or a local members' Group who may run an associate scheme for motorcyclists.

What do I get?

If you did not reach the standard which the IAM seeks for membership, the examiner will give you a detailed verbal report at the end of the test backed up by a written statement of any faults revealed during tests. It is worth remembering that if you have a riding fault it is better you should know about it before it finds you out? The written report should enable you to improve your riding technique.

If successful in the test, the examiner will give you a temporary certificate and will recommend you to the Institute's Council for election. Subsequently, a permanent certificate will be issued to you, and you will be able to purchase and display the distinctive IAM badge which you have earned. Subject to a satisfactory proposal, you may also avail yourself of a special motorcycle insurance policy underwritten at Lloyd's. The special terms include a 10 per cent discount for IAM membership, comprehensive cover even for riders under 25 years of age, and a 30 per cent no claims bonus after 3 years.

As a member you will also receive *Milestones* magazine and by joining a local members' Group you will have a chance to meet other members and take part in safety activities in your area and any social events which they organise.

However, most important of all you will be able to make a positive contribution to our accident problems by your own conduct, by encouraging others to improve their standards, by making good riding fashionable.

Why not put your abilities to the test by filling out the application form on the pages 121–6.

Quick change

Not long ago, astonished police found a motorist trying to change a wheel – in the outside lane of the M1 in Northamptonshire.

Horror story

When Danny McInulty was a young police officer at the opening of the M3, he saw that motorway's first horror story: 'Two elderly gentlemen had a collision in the middle lane, got out of their cars and stood there solemnly exchanging details on the motorway.'

14

WHY DO SOME DRIVERS FAIL THE TEST?

Listed below are the main reasons, but remember that few of the faults listed would by themselves have been sufficient to bring about failure. We have analysed only the unsuccessful candidates but it should be remembered that those who did reach the standard made their mistakes too. We have yet to test the perfect driver.

78% Hazard procedure and cornering: Incorrect assessment. Poor safety margin. Unsystematic procedure.
72% Use of gears: Late selection. Intermediate gears not used to advantage.
70% Positioning: Straddles lanes. Incorrect for right and left turns.
60% Braking: Late brake application. Harsh handbrake application. Brake and change gear simultaneously.
58% Distance observation: Late planning and assessment of traffic conditions
48% Method of approach: Too fast approach. Coasted to compulsory stops. Offside at 'Keep left' sign.
48% Clutch control: Ride clutch. Clutch slip. Coasting.
40% Car sympathy: Not expressed in use of clutch, brakes and gears.
38% Traffic observation: Poor anticipation. Late reaction.
36% Observation and obedience: Failed to remember signs when requested. Failure to conform to 'Stop' signs and/or 'Keep left' signs.
33% Overtaking: Too close prior to overtaking. On bends. In face of approaching traffic. Cutting in after overtaking.

28% Manoeuvring and reversing: Lacked in judgement and control.

26% Correct use of speed: Excessive in country lanes. Failed to make adequate progress in 70 mph areas.

22% Speed limits: Exceeding speed limits.

20% Steering: Released wheel. Crossed hands.

20% Restraint: Insufficient restraint demonstrated.

14% Maintaining adequate progress: Not maintained when safe to make progress.

14% Hand or mechanical signals: Late or misleading signals.

14% Correct use of horn: Failed to use when required.

12% Acceleration: Uneven – poor acceleration sense.

8% Obstructing other vehicles: Loitering at minor hazards, also cutting in.

Squeaky

Parts of the M5 near Weston-super-Mare, Avon, have been edged with squeaky surfaces to alert holiday drivers who nod off during long journeys.

15

SPECIALISED FLEET TRAINING

Why Fleet training?

1 Your company vehicle fleet represents a high capital outlay.
2 The drivers of those vehicles are a vital link in the performance of your company as a whole.
3 You need to obtain maximum cost effectiveness from your vehicles and the staff employed to use them.

An employee who has had training in the operation and understanding of a vehicle is less likely to incur costs. Staff trained in driving skills will be safer drivers and are less likely to be off work as a result of an accident.

Not only are your accident damage costs likely to fall but your insurance costs as well. Down-time will also be reduced.

What is IAM Fleet Training?

As a result of the experience of the Institute of Advanced Motorists in dealing with fleet operators we have now established a specialist organisation: IAM Fleet Training Ltd. Training is based on the highly successful driving system set out in the Police 'Roadcraft' manual.

Courses will be under the direction of former senior police driving instructors who have a very broad range of training experience in vehicles ranging from motorcycles to articulated lorries.

What training courses do we offer?

A wide variety from a one-day course at your own premises with your own vehicles to a week's course at a training establishment with accommodation and vehicles provided. Courses can be tailor-made to meet precisely your company's needs. Individual assessment reports will be provided to management at no extra cost.

Does it work?

By teaching 'Roadcraft' methods, the Hendon Police School was able to reduce accidents from 1 in 9,000 miles run to 1 in 25,000 miles run, and subsequently this accident rate fell to 1 in 72,587 miles run. Using the same principles, assessments will show how to overcome any adverse habits and incorrect techniques, in addition to making a positive contribution to improved driving skills.

A TRRL Report (LR 49) disclosed that qualified advanced motorists had an average of between 50 per cent and 75 per cent fewer accidents than motorists who had not followed the IAM programme.

What does it cost?

Very little when you consider the expense of even a minor accident. Save that cost and the IAM Fleet Training programme will have paid for itself. Why not contact us for more details and a quotation by getting in touch with:

The Managing Director, IAM Fleet Training Ltd
1a Marlborough Road, Chiswick, London W4 4EU
Telephone: 01-994 4403

First casualty

The first casualty on any motorway in Britain was Harold Bradshaw, seriously injured when he fell from a bridge on to the Preston by-pass just four hours after it was opened.

PART THREE
APPENDICES

APPENDIX I

STATUTORY INSTRUMENTS
1982 No. 1163 ROAD TRAFFIC SPECIAL ROADS
The Motorways Traffic (England and Wales) Regulations 1982
Made: 11th August, 1982. Laid before Parliament 24th August 1982.
Coming into Operation 15th September 1982.

The Secretary of State for Transport (as respects England) and the Secretary of State for Wales (as respects Wales), in exercise of the powers conferred by Section 13(2) and (3) of the Road Traffic Regulations Act 1967 and now vested in them, and of all other enabling powers, and after consultation with representative organisations in accordance with the provisions of section 107(2) of that Act, hereby makes the following Regulations:

Commencement and citation
1 These Regulations shall come into operation on 15th September 1982 and may be cited as the Motorways Traffic (England and Wales) Regulations 1982.

Revocation
2 The Motorways Traffic Regulations 1959 and the Motorways Traffic (England and Wales) (Amendment) Regulations 1971 are hereby revoked.

Interpretation
3 (1) In these Regulations, the following expressions have the meanings hereby respectively assigned to them:

(a) 'the Act of 1967' means the Road Traffic Regulation Act 1967

(b) 'carriageway' means that part of a motorway which –

(i) is constructed with a surface suitable for the regular passage of vehicular motor traffic along the motorway.

(ii) has on each side either a hard shoulder, a raised kerb, or a central reservation, and

(iii) has the approximate position of its edges marked with a traffic sign of the type shown in diagram 1012.1 in Schedule 2 to the Traffic Signs Regulations and General Directions 1981;

(c) 'central reservation' means that part of a motorway which separates the carriageway to be used by vehicles travelling in one direction from the carriageway to be used by vehicles travelling in the opposite direction;

(d) 'excluded traffic' means traffic which is not traffic of Classes I or II;

(e) 'hard shoulder' means a part of the motorway which is adjacent to and situated on the left hand or near side of the carriageway when facing in the direction in which vehicles may be driven in accordance with Regulation 6, and which is designed to take the weight of a vehicle;

(*f*) 'motorway' means any road or part of a road to which these Regulations apply by virtue of Regulation 4;

(*g*) 'verge' means any part of a motorway which is not a carriageway, a hard shoulder, or a central reservation.

(2) A vehicle shall be treated for the purposes of any provision of these Regulations as being on any part of a motorway specified in that provision if any part of the vehicle (whether it is at rest or not) is on the part of the motorway so specified.

(3) Any provision of these Regulations containing any prohibition or restriction relating to the driving, moving or stopping of a vehicle, or to its remaining at rest, shall be construed as a provision that no person shall use a motorway by driving, moving or stopping the vehicle or by causing or permitting it to be driven or moved, or to stop or remain at rest, in contravention of that prohibition or restriction.

(4) In these Regulations references to numbered classes of traffic are references to the classes of traffic set out in Schedule 4 to the Highways Act 1980.

Application
4 These regulations apply to every special road or part of a special road which can only be used by traffic of Classes I or II, but shall not apply to any part of any such road until such dates as may be declared in accordance with the provisions of section 1(7) of the Act of 1967 to be the date on which it is open for use as a special road.

Vehicles to be driven on the carriageways only
5 Subject to the following provisions of these Regulations, no vehicle shall be driven on any part of a motorway which is not a carriageway.

Direction of driving
6 (1) Where there is a traffic sign indicating that there is no entry to a carriageway at a particular place, no vehicle shall be driven or moved onto that carriage at that place.

(2) Where there is a traffic sign indicating that there is no left or right turn into a carriageway at a particular place, no vehicle shall be so driven or moved as to cause it to turn to the left or (as the case may be) to the right into that carriageway at that place.

(3) Every vehicle on a length of carriageway which is contiguous to a central reservation shall be driven in such a direction that the central reservation is at all times on the right hand or off side of the vehicle.

(4) Where traffic signs are so placed that there is a length of carriageway (being a length which is not contiguous to a central reservation) which can be entered at one end only by vehicles driven in conformity with paragraph (1) of this Regulation, every vehicle on that length of carriageway shall be driven in such a direction only as to cause it to proceed away from that end of that length of carriageway towards the other end thereof.

(5) Without prejudice to the foregoing provisions of this Regulation, no vehicle which

(*a*) is on a length of carriageway on which vehicles are required by any of the foregoing provisions of this Regulation to be driven in one direction only and is proceeding in or facing that direction, or *(b)* is on any length of carriageway and is proceeding in or facing one direction

shall be driven or moved so as to cause it to turn and proceed in or face the opposite direction.

Restriction on stopping
7 (1) Subject to the following provisions of this Regulation, no vehicle shall stop or remain at rest on a carriageway.

(2) Where it is necessary for a vehicle which is being driven on a carriageway to be stopped while it is on a motorway –

(a) by reason of a breakdown or mechanical defect or lack of fuel, oil or water, required for the vehicle; or

(b) by reason of any accident, illness or other emergency; or

(c) to permit any person carried in or on the vehicle to recover or move any object which has fallen onto a motorway; or

(d) to permit any person carried in or on the vehicle to give help which is required by any other person in any of the circumstances specified in the foregoing provisions of this paragraph,

the vehicle shall, as soon and in so far as is reasonably practicable, be driven or moved off the carriageway on to, and may stop and remain at rest on, any hard shoulder which is contiguous to that carriageway.

(3) *(a)* A vehicle which is at rest on a hard shoulder shall so far as is reasonably practicable be allowed to remain at rest on that hard shoulder in such a position only that no part of it or of the load carried thereby shall obstruct or be a cause of danger to vehicles using the carriageway.

(b) A vehicle shall not remain at rest on a hard shoulder for longer than is necessary in the circumstances or for the purposes specified in paragraph 2 of this Regulation.

(4) Nothing in the foregoing provisions of this Regulation shall preclude a vehicle from stopping or remaining at rest on a carriageway while it is prevented from proceeding along the carriageway by the presence of any other vehicle or any person or object.

Restriction on reversing
8 No vehicle on a motorway shall be driven or moved backwards except in so far as it is necessary to back the vehicle to enable it to proceed forwards or to be connected to any other vehicle.

Restriction on use of hard shoulders
9 No vehicle shall be driven or stop or remain at rest on any hard shoulder except in accordance with paragraphs (2) and (3) of Regulation 7.

Vehicles not to use the central reservation or verge
10 No vehicle shall be driven or moved or stop or remain at rest on a central reservation or verge.

Vehicles not to be driven by learner drivers
11 No motor vehicle shall be driven on a motorway by a person who is authorised to drive that vehicle only by virtue of his being the holder of a

provisional licence under section 88(2) of the Road Traffic Act 1972, unless, since the date of coming into force of the said provisional licence that person has passed a test prescribed under section 85 of the Road Traffic Act 1972 sufficient to entitle him under that Act to be granted a licence, other than a provisional licence, authorising him to drive that vehicle on a road.

Restriction on use of right hand or off side lane

12) (1) This Regulation applies to –

(a) a motor car with a maximum gross weight exceeding 7.5 tonnes,

(b) a heavy motor car, except a heavy motor car constructed solely for the carriage of passengers and their effects and not adapted or used for any other purpose the overall length of which does not exceed 12 metres, and

(c) a motor vehicle drawing a trailer.

(2) Subject to the provisions of paragraph (3) below, no vehicle to which this Regulation applies shall be driven, or moved, or stop or remain at rest on the right hand or off side lane of a length of carriageway which has three or more traffic lanes at any place where all the lanes are open for use by traffic proceeding in the same direction.

(3) The prohibition contained in paragraph (2) above shall not apply to a vehicle while it is being driven on any right hand or off side lane such as is mentioned in that paragraph in so far as it is necessary for the vehicle to be so driven to enable it to pass another vehicle which is carrying or drawing a load of exceptional width.

(4) In this Regulation –

(a) 'maximum gross weight' has the same meaning as in Regulation 4 of the Traffic Signs Regulations and General Directions 1981; and

(b) 'overall length' has the same meaning as in Regulation 3(1) of the Motor Vehicles (Construction and Use) Regulations 1978.

Restrictions affecting persons on foot on a motorway

13 No person shall at any time while on foot go or remain on any part of a motorway other than a hard should except in so far as it is necessary for him to do so to reach a hard shoulder or to secure compliance with any of these Regulations or to recover or remove any object which has fallen on to a motorway or to give help which is required by any other person in any of the circumstances specified in paragraph (2) of Regulation 7.

Restrictions affecting animals carried in vehicles

14 The person in charge of any animal which is carried by a vehicle using a motorway shall, so far as is practicable, secure that –

(a) the animal shall not be removed from or permitted to leave the vehicle while the vehicle is on a motorway, and

(b) if it escapes from, or it is necessary for it to be removed from, or permitted to leave, the vehicle –

(i) it shall not go or remain on any part of a motorway other than a hard shoulder, and

(ii) it shall whilst it is not on or in the vehicle be held on a lead or otherwise kept under proper control.

Use of motorway by excluded traffic

15 Excluded traffic is hereby authorised to use a motorway on the occasions or in the emergencies and to the extent specified in the following provisions of this paragraph, that is to say –

(a) traffic of Classes III or IV may use a motorway for the maintenance, repair, cleaning or clearance of any part of a motorway or for the erection, laying, placing, maintenance, testing, alteration, repair or removal of any structure, works or apparatus in, on, under or over any part of a motorway;

(b) pedestrians may use a motorway –

(i) when it is necessary for them to do so as a result of an accident or emergency or of a vehicle being at rest on a motorway in any of the circumstances specified in paragraph (2) of Regulation 7, or

(ii) in any of the circumstances specified in sub paragraphs (b), (d), (e) or (f) of paragraph (1) of Regulation 16.

(2) The Secretary of State may authorise the use of a motorway by any excluded traffic on occasion or in emergency or for the purpose of enabling such traffic to cross a motorway or to secure access to premises abutting on or adjacent to a motorway.

(3) Where by reason of any emergency the use of any road (not being a motorway) by any excluded traffic is rendered impossible or unsuitable the Chief Officer of Police of the police area in which a motorway or any part of a motorway is situated, or any officer of or above the rank of superintendent authorised in that behalf by that Chief Officer, may –

(a) authorise any excluded traffic to use that motorway or that part of a motorway as an alternative road for the period during which the use of the other road by such traffic continues to be impossible or unsuitable, and

(b) relax any prohibition or restriction imposed by these Regulations in so far as he considers it necessary to do so in connection with the use of that motorway or that part of a motorway by excluded traffic in pursuance of any such authorisation as aforesaid.

Exceptions and relaxations

16 (1) nothing in the foregoing provisions of these Regulations shall preclude any person from using a motorway otherwise than in accordance with the provisions in any of the following circumstances, that is to say –

(a) where he does so in accordance with any direction or permission given by a constable in uniform or with the indication given by a traffic sign;

(b) where, in accordance with any permisison given by a constable, he does so for the purpose or investigating any accident which has occurred on or near a motorway;

(c) where it is necessary for him to do so to avoid or prevent an accident or to obtain or give help required as the result of an accident or emergency, and he does so in such manner as to cause as little danger or inconvenience as possible to other traffic on a motorway;

(d) where he does so in the exercise of his duty as a constable or as a member of a fire brigade or of an ambulance service;

(*e*) where it is necessary for him to do so to carry out in an efficient manner –

(i) the maintenance, repair, cleaning, clearance, alteration or improvement of any part of a motorway, or

(ii) the removal of any vehicle from any part of a motorway, or

(iii) the erection, laying, placing, maintenance, testing alteration, repair or removal of any structure, works or apparatus in, on, under or over any part of a motorway; or

(*f*) where it is necessary for him to do so in connection with any inspection, survey, investigation or census which is carried out in accordance with any general or special authority granted by the Secretary of State.

(2) Without prejudice to the foregoing provisions of these regulations, the Secretary of State may relax any prohibition or restriction imposed by these Regulations.

4th August 1982. David Howell, Secretary of State for Transport,
Signed by authority of the Secretary of State 11th August 1982. Michael Roberts, Parliamentary Under Secretary of State, Welsh Office.

EXPLANATORY NOTE
(This Note is not part of the Regulations)

These Regulations revoke and re-enact with amendments the provisions of The Motorways Traffic Regulations 1959 and The Motorways Traffic (England and Wales) (Amendment) Regulations 1971.

The principal amendments are as follows –

(1) The definitions of the constituent parts of a motorway in Regulation 3(1) are amended, introducing a specific definition of hard shoulder in Regulation 3(1)*(e)*. The provisions in Regulations 7 and 9 as to stopping on a motorway are, in consequence, framed by reference to the hard shoulder.

(2) The restrictions on the use of the right hand or offside lane are amended so that they apply to a motor car with a maximum gross weight exceeding 7.5 tonnes, and a heavy motor car constructed for the carriage of passengers and their effects and which has an overall length greater than 12 metres (Regulation 12[1]). These restrictions will apply on any motorway which has three or more traffic lanes where all the lanes are open for use by traffic proceeding in the same directions (Regulation 12[2]).

APPENDIX II

MOTORWAYS TRAFFIC (SCOTLAND) REGULATIONS, 1964

(Made under Section 17, Road Traffic Regulation Act, 1984)
**Note: For penalty for a contravention of these Regulations,
see Schedule 7, Road Traffic Regulation Act, 1984.**

Interpretation

(2) In these Regulations, unless the context otherwise requires, the following expressions have the meanings hereby respectively assigned to them, that is to say –

(a) 'carriageway' means that part of a motorway which is constructed with a surface suitable for the regular passage of vehicular motor traffic along the motorway and is distinguishable from the other parts of the motorway by the fact that on each side that part of the motorway either consists of a marginal strip or is contiguous to a raised kerb, but the said expression does not include any part of a central reservation;

(b) 'central reservation' means that part of a motorway which separates two carriageways running along that motorway parallel or approximately parallel to each other and which is contiguous on one side to one of those carriageways and on the other side to the other of those carriageways.

(c) 'excluded traffic' means traffic which is not traffic of Classes I or II;

(d) 'marginal strip' means a continuous strip of the surface of a carriageway which is at the side of that carriageway and is distinguishable from the rest of that surface by having a colour which is different from the colour of the rest of that surface;

(e) 'the Secretary of State' means the Secretary of State for Scotland;

(f) 'motorway' means any road or part of a road to which these Regulations apply by virtue of Regulation 3;

(g) 'traffic sign' has the meaning assigned thereto by Section 64(1), Road Traffic Regulation Act, 1984;

(h) 'verge' means any part of a motorway which is not a carriageway or a central reservation.

(3) A vehicle shall be treated for the purposes of any provision of these regulations as being on any part of a motorway specified in that provision if any part of the vehicle (whether it is at rest or not) is on the part of the motorway so specified.

(4) Any provision of these Regulations containing any prohibition or restriction relating to the driving, moving or stopping of a vehicle, or to its remaining at rest, shall be construed as a provision that no person shall use a motorway by driving,

moving or stopping the vehicle or by causing or permitting it to be driven or moved, or to stop or remain at rest, in contravention of that prohibition or restriction.

(5) In these Regulations references to numbered classes of traffic are references to the classes of traffic of those numbers set out in Schedule 3 to the Roads (Scotland) Act, 1984, or, as for the time being varied or amended by virtue of any order made by the Secretary of State under Section 8 of that Act (Regulation 2).

The Motorways
These Regulations apply to every special road or part of a special road provided in pursuance of a scheme made or confirmed by the Secretary of State under Section 7, Roads (Scotland) Act, 1984, being a road or, as the case may be, a part of a road which (save as otherwise provided by or under Regulations made under Section 17, Road Traffic Regulation Act, 1984) can only be used by traffic of Classes I or II.

Notes: The phrase in brackets would apear to refer to these Regulations.

Provided that these Regulations shall not aply to any part of any such road until such date as may be declared in accordance with Section 17(5) and (6), Road Traffic Regulation Act, 1984, to be the date on which it is open for use as a special road (Regulation 3).

Notes: Section 17(5) is not reproduced, but the date on which a road or any part thereof is open for use as a special road shall, not less than 7 days before that date, be published in at least one newspaper circulating in the area in which the special road or, as in the case may be, that part of the road, is situated, and in the *Edinburgh Gazette (Regulation 3, Special Roads [Notice of Opening] [Scotland] Regulations, 1964).*

Vehicles to be Driven on the Carriageways Only
Subject to the following provisions of the Regulations, no vehicle shall be driven on any part of a motorway which is not a carriageway (Regulation 4).

Direction of Driving
(1) Where there is a traffic sign indicating that there is no entry to a carriageway at a particular place, no vehicle shall be driven or moved on to that carriageway at that place.

(2) Where there is a traffic sign indicating that there is no left or right turn into a carriageway at a particular place, no vehicle shall be so driven or moved as to cause it to turn to the left or (as the case may be) to the right into that carriageway at that place.

(3) Every vehicle on a length of carriageway which is contiguous to a central reservation shall be driven in such a direction that that reservation is at all times on the right hand or off side of the vehicle.

(4) Where traffic signs are so placed that there is a length of carriageway (being a length which is not contiguous to a central reservation) which can be entered at one end only by vehicles driven in conformity with paragraph (1) of this regulation, every vehicle on that length of carriageway shall be driven in such a direction only as to cause it to proceed away from that end of that length of carriageway towards the other end thereof.

(5) Without prejudice to the foregoing provisions of this Regulation, no vehicle which

(a) is on a length of carriageway on which vehicles are required by any of the foregoing provisions of this Regulation to be driven in one direction only and is proceeding in or facing that direction, or

(b) is on any other length of carriageway and is proceeding in or facing one direction

shall be driven or moved so as to cause it to turn and proceed in or face the opposite direction (Regulation 5).

Restrictions on Stopping

(1) Subject to the following provisions of this Regulation, no vehicle shall stop or remain at rest on a carriageway.

(2) Where it is necessary for a vehicle which is being driven on a carriageway to be stopped while it is on a motorway –
    (a) by reason of a breakdown or mechanical defect or lack of fuel, oil or water required for the vehicle; or

    (b) by reason of any accident, illness or other emergency; or

    (c) to permit any person carried in or on the vehicle to recover or move any object which has fallen on a motorway; or

    (d) to permit any person carried in or on the vehicle to give help which is required by any other person in any of the circumstances specified in the foregoing provisions of this paragraph,

the vehicle shall, as soon as in so far as is reasonably practicable, be driven or moved off the carriageway on to, and may stop and remain at rest on, the verge which lies on the left hand or near side of that vehicle while it is proceeding along that carriageway in accordance with the provisions of Regulations 5.

(3) A vehicle which is at rest on a verge in any of the circumstances specified in paragraph (2) of this Regulation –
    (a) shall so far as is reasonably practicable be allowed to remain at rest on that verge in such a position only that no part of it or of the load carried thereby shall obstruct or be a cause of danger to vehicles using the carriageway, and

    (b) shall not remain at rest on that verge for longer than is necessary in those circumstances.

(4) Nothing in the foregoing provisions of this Regulation shall preclude a vehicle from stopping or remaining at rest on a carriageway while it is prevented from proceeding along that carriageway by the presence of any other vehicle or any person or object (Regulation 6).

Restrictions on Reversing

No vehicle on a carriageway shall be driven or moved backwards except in so far as it is necessary to back the vehicle to enable it to proceed forward along the carriageway or to be connected to any other vehicle (Regulation 7).

Restrictions on Use of Verges

No vehicle shall be driven or moved or stop or remain at rest on any verge except in accordance with Regulation 6(2) and (3) (Regulation 8).

Vehicles not to Use the Central Reservation

No vehicle shall be driven or moved or stop or remain at rest on a central reservation (Regulation 9).

Vehicles not to be Driven by Learner Drivers
No motor vehicle shall be driven on a motorway by a person who is authorised to drive that vehicle on a road by virtue only of his being the holder of a provisional licence granted to him under Section 89(1), Road Traffic Act, 1972:
    Provided that this Regulation shall not apply to a vehicle which is being driven on a motorway by a person authorised as aforesaid if that person has, since the date of coming into force of the said provisional licence, passed a test prescribed under Section 85(2) of the said Act of 1972, sufficient to entitle him to be granted under that Act a licence, other than a provisional licence, authorising him to drive that vehicle on a road. (Regulation 10).

Notes: A 'learner driver' who holds an expired provisional licence would be dealt with for a contravention of section 84(1), Road Traffic Act, 1972, and not under this Regulation.

Restriction on Use of Right-Hand or Off-Side Lane

(1) This regulation applies to –

(a) a motor vehicle other than –

(i) a motor car with an unladen weight not exceeding 3 tons;

(ii) a heavy motor car constructed solely for the carriage of passengers and their effects and not adapted or used for any other purpose; or

(iii) a motorcycle; and

(b) a motor vehicle drawing a trailer.

(2) No vehicle to which this regulation applies shall be driven or moved, nor shall it stop or remain at rest, on the right hand or off side lane of any length of carriageway which has three traffic lanes at any place where all three lanes are open for use by traffic proceeding in the same direction:
    Provided that this prohibition shall not apply to any vehicle while it is being driven on the right hand or off side lane in order to pass another vehicle which is carrying or drawing a load of such exceptional width that that vehicle can pass it only if it is driven on the right hand or off side lane. (Regulation 10A, as inserted by [Amendment] Regulations, 1968).

Restrictions Affecting Persons on Foot on a Motorway
No person shall at any time while on foot go or remain on any part of a motorway other than a verge except in so far as it is necessary for him to do so to get to a verge or to secure compliance with any of these regulations or to recover or move an object which has fallen on a motorway or to give help which is required by any other person in any of the circumstances specified in Regulation 6(2) (Regulation 11).

Restrictions Affecting Animals Carried in Vehicles
The person in charge of any animal which is carried by a vehicle using a motorway shall, so far as is practicable, secure that –

(a) the animal shall not be removed from or permitted to leave the vehicle while the vehicle is on the motorway, and

(b) if it escapes from, or it is necessary for it to be removed from, or permitted to leave, the vehicle –

(i) it shall not go or remain on any part of a motorway other than a verge, and

(ii) it shall whilst it is not on or in the vehicle be held on a lead or otherwise kept under proper control (Regulation 12).

Use of Motorway by Excluded Traffic
(1) Excluded traffic is hereby authorised to use a motorway on the occasions or in the emergencies and to the extent specified in the following provisions of this paragraph, that is to say –

(a) traffic of Classes III or IV may use a motorway for the maintenance, repair, cleaning or clearance of any part of a motorway or for the erection, laying, placing, maintenance, testing, alteration, repair or removal of any structure, works or apparatus in, on, under or over any part of the motorway;

(b) pedestrians may use a motorway –

(i) when it is necessary for them to do so as a result of an accident or emergency or of a vehicle being at rest on a motorway in any of the circumstances specified in Regulation 6(2), or

(ii) in any of the circumstances specified in Regulation 14(1) (b), (d), (e) or (f).

(2) Without prejudice to the foregoing provisions of the Regulation, the Secretary of State may authorise the use of a motorway by any excluded traffic on occasion or in emergency or for the purpose of enabling such traffic to cross a motorway or to secure access to premises abutting on or adjacent to a motorway.

(3) Without prejudice to the foregoing provisions of this Regulation, where by reason of any emergency the use of any road (not being a motorway) by any excluded traffic is rendered impossible or unsuitable the Chief Constable of the police area in which a motorway or any part of a motorway is situated, or any office of or above the rank of Superintendent authorised in that behalf by that Chief Constable, may –

(a) authorise any excluded traffic to use that motorway or that part of a motorway as an alternative road for the period during which the use of the other road by such traffic continues to be impossible or unsuitable, and

(b) relax any prohibition or restriction imposed by these regulations in so far as he considers it necessary to do so in connection with the use of that motorway or that part of a motorway by excluded traffic in pursuance of any such authorisation as aforesaid (Regulation 13).

Notes: For classes of traffic, see Regulation 2(5) herein and Note thereunder.

Exceptions and Relaxations
(1) Nothing in the foregoing provisions of these Regulations shall preclude any person from using a motorway otherwise than in accordance with those provisions in any of the following circumstances, that is to say –

(a) where he does so in accordance with any direction or permission given by a constable in uniform or with the indication given by a traffic sign;

(b) where he does so in accordance with any permission given by a constable and for the purpose of investigating any accident which has occurred on or near a motorway;

(c) where –

(i) it is necessary for him to do so to avoid or prevent an accident or to obtain or give help required as the result of an accident or emergency, and

(ii) he does so in such manner as to cause as little danger or inconvenience as possible to other traffic on a motorway;

(d) where he does so in the exercise of his duty as a constable or as a member of a fire brigade or of an ambulance service;

(e) where it is necessary for him to do so to carry out in an efficient manner –

(i) the maintenance, repair, cleaning, clearance, alteration or improvement of any part of a motorway, or

(iii) the removal of any vehicle from any part of a motorway or

(iii) the erection, laying, placing, maintenance, testing, alteration, repair or removal of any structure, works or apparatus in, on, under or over any part of a motorway; or

(f) where it is necessary for him to do so in connection with any inspection, survey, investigation or census which relates to a motorway or any part thereof and which is carried out in accordance with any general or special authority granted by the Secretary of State (Regulation 14).

APPENDIX III APPLICATION FORMS

Application form for Advanced Driving Test

FOR OFFICE USE ONLY

D	
T	
R	
E	

To: The Secretary
INSTITUTE OF ADVANCED MOTORISTS
359 CHISWICK HIGH ROAD, LONDON W4 4HS
Telephone: 01-994 4403 (24-hour answering service) FAX (01) 994 9249

Application for Advanced Driving Test and admission to Membership of the Institute

Please give the following particulars in block capitals

If already a member, please give Membership Number ☐☐☐☐☐☐☐

1. Surname (Mr/Mrs/Miss) ....

2. Christian name(s) in full ....

3. Year of Birth ....   3a. Occupation ....

4. Address ....

....

....   Postcode ....

5. Tel. No. ....   Business.......................................

6a. Has any Court in the last three years ordered a conviction to be endorsed on your licence? (This includes an order for disqualification.) If not, please write 'No' below. If answer is 'Yes' please give following particulars for consideration by Council before acceptance. Read Note (A).

Offence ....

Date of conviction ....

Penalty ....

6b. Are there any Proceedings pending? ....

    If so, for what offence? ....

7.   Date of expiry of current driving licence ....
Holders of a Provisional or Visitor's licence are not eligible.

8.   On what vehicle do you propose to be tested?

....

Make and model ....

Year ....   Registration No ....

9a. Is this vehicle covered by insurance against third party risk? ....

Name of insurance company ....

9b. If the vehicle is not insured by you personally but, for
instance, you are employed under a block scheme, give
particulars, or name of person from whom particulars
can be obtained.

....

Please complete the following statement:

10a. I hereby apply to undergo the advanced driving test, which I understand
will be of not less than one and a half hours' duration and will be arranged at a
mutually convenient time and place (normally 14 days' notice is required).

(b) Date and test route required ....

Morning/Afternoon (*Please cross out time not applicable*)

Alternative dates

1 ....   2 ....3 ....4 ....

(c)   If successful in the Test I hereby apply for admission to Membership of the
Institute of Advanced Motorists, for which I understand the annual subscription
is £7.50 which will make me eligible for any benefits. If already a member, an
additional certificate can be obtained for £1.

(d)   I enclose £26.00, being £18.50 as the fee for the test and £7.50 as my first
annual subscription as a member of the Institute, which latter sum will, I
understand, be refunded to me if I am unsuccessful in the Test. Read Note (B). If
already a member, a test fee of £18.50 only is payable.

I authorise you to debit my Access/Barclaycard account with the amount of

....   My credit card number is ....

(e)   I undertake when attending the Test to produce my current Driving Licence
and Certificate of Insurance or other evidence. Read Note (C).

(f)   I declare that to the best of my knowledge and belief the answers given
above are true.

(g)   I agree that the Institute and its officers and employees shall not be under any liability for any injury, damage or loss whatever and however caused; and that I am bound by the Articles of Association of the Institute and any of its Rules and Regulations lawfully made from time to time.

Date ....   Usual signature ....

NOTES:

(A)   If you have been disqualified by a Court and the period of disqualification expired at any time within the last three years, please give particulars of the disqualification, in answer to question 6, although the Order of the Court may have been made more than three years ago.

(B)   Cheques and Postal Orders should be made payable to 'The Institute of Advanced Motorists' and crossed. Coin or bank notes should be sent by registered post. Annual payments after the first year can be conveniently made by banker's order.

(C)   The words 'other evidence' in 10(e) refer to question 9(b) and apply to cases where the applicant, by reason of being insured under a block scheme, cannot produce a personal Certificate of Insurance.

(D)   For other terms and conditions and other details please see the Institute's brochure.

VAT No. 222/5170/05

Application form for Solo Motorcycle Test

SMC

D	
T	
R	
E	

FOR OFFICE USE ONLY

To: The Secretary
INSTITUTE OF ADVANCED MOTORISTS
359 CHISWICK HIGH ROAD, LONDON W4 4HS
Telephone: 01-994 4403 (24-hour answering service) FAX (01) 994 9249

**Application for SOLO MOTORCYCLE TEST and admission to
Membership of the Institute**

The test is subject to the following conditions:

1. Must be in the 200cc Class or above
2. Helmet and goggles, or helmet with visor incorporated, and gloves, must be worn whilst riding.
3. Machine must be in a roadworthy condition.
4. Applicant must hold a full driving licence.

THE INSTITUTE OF ADVANCED MOTORISTS RESERVE THE RIGHT TO DECLINE TO CONDUCT A TEST IF THESE CONDITIONS ARE NOT COMPLIED WITH.

Please give the following particulars in block capitals

If already a member, please give Membership Number ☐☐☐☐☐☐

1. Surname (Mr/Mrs/Miss) ....

2. Christian name(s) in full ....

3. Year of Birth .... 3a. Occupation ....

4. Address ....

....

.... Postcode ....

5. Tel. No. .... Business...

6a. Has any Court in the last three years ordered a conviction to be endorsed on your licence? (This includes an order for disqualification.) If not, please write 'No' below. If answer is 'Yes' please give following particulars for consideration by Council before acceptance. Read Note (A).

Offence ....

Date of conviction ....

Penalty ....

6b. Are there any Proceedings pending? ....

7. Date of expiry of current driving licence ....
   Holders of a Provisional or Visitor's licence are not eligible.

8. On what vehicle do you propose to be tested?

....

Make and type ....

Registration number ....

Age .... Cubic capacity cc

9a. Is this vehicle covered by insurance against third party risk? ....

Name of insurance company ....

9b. If the vehicle is not insured by you personally but, for
instance, you are employed under a block scheme, give
particulars, or name of person from whom particulars
can be obtained.

Please complete the following statement:
10a. I hereby apply to undergo the advanced driving test, which I understand
will be of not less than one and a half hours' duration and will be arranged at
a mutually convenient time and place (normally 14 days' notice is required).

(b) Once the test application is received at the Institute, a photostat copy will
be forwarded to the examiner. He will then contact the candidate to make a
mutually acceptable date and time for the test. Please state route required.

Route ....

(c) If successful in the Test I hereby apply for admission to Membership of
the Institute of Advanced Motorists, for which I understand the annual
subscription is £7.50 which will make me eligible for any benefits. If already a
member, an additional certificate can be obtained for £1.

(d) I enclose £26.00, being £18.50 as the fee for the test and £7.50 as my first
annual subscription as a member of the Institute, which latter sum will, I
understand, be refunded to me if I am unsuccessful in the Test. Read Note
(B). If already a member, a test fee of £18.50 only is payable.

I authorise you to debit my Access/Barclaycard account with the amount of

.... My credit card number is ....

(e) I undertake when attending the Test to produce my current Driving
Licence and Certificate of Insurance or other evidence. Read Note (C).

(f) I declare that to the best of my knowledge and belief the answers given
above are true.

(g) I agree that the Institute and its officers and employees shall not be
under any liability for any injury, damage or loss whatever and however
caused; and that I am bound by the Articles of Association of the Institute and
any of its Rules and Regulations lawfully made from time to time.

Date .... Usual signature ....

NOTES:

(A)   If you have been disqualified by a Court and the period of disqualification expired at any time within the last three years, please give particulars of the disqualification, in answer to question 6, although the Order of the Court may have been made more than three years ago.

(B)   Cheques and Postal Orders should be made payable to 'The Institute of Advanced Motorists' and crossed. Coin or bank notes should be sent by registered post. Annual payments after the first year can be conveniently made by banker's order.

(C)   The words 'other evidence' in 10(e) refer to question 9(b) and apply to cases where the applicant, by reason of being insured under a block scheme, cannot produce a personal Certificate of Insurance.

(D)   For other terms and conditions and other details please see the Institute's brochure.

VAT No. 222/5170/05

OTHER IAM AND KOGAN PAGE PUBLICATIONS

Advanced Motoring
third edition

This well-known and concisely written manual, now fully revised and updated, is intended to encourage all motorists to achieve a high standard of driving. It is based on the advanced driving methods taught by the Institute of Advanced Motorists' examiners who are all former Class One police drivers.

It gives expert advice and practical down-to-earth information on every aspect of improving your driving skills. For anyone preparing for the Institute's advanced driving test this book is essential reading. It explains what is meant by the Institute's motto 'Skill with Responsibility'.

Paperback   ISBN 1 85091 913 5   216 x 135 mm   156 pages

Advanced Motorcycling
second edition

The second edition of this popular book, now fully revised and updated, provides a readable and practical guide for all motorcyclists, ranging from the experienced rider who is considering taking the Institute's advanced test to the novice seeking basic instruction on safe driving. It contains a wealth of information and specialist knowledge on every aspect of travelling on two wheels.

Paperback   ISBN 1 85091 914 3   216 x 135 mm   156 pages